CONTEMPLATING WITH

Loyev Books

CONTEMPLATING WITH ANCIENT PHILOSOPHERS

A "Deep Philosophy" approach to thinkers of the past

by
Ran Lahav

Design and Drawings by Karin Fechner

Loyev Books

Hardwick, Vermont, USA

https://dphilo.org/books

Loyev Books

1165 Hopkins Hill Rd., Hardwick, Vermont 05843, USA

https://dphilo.org/books

9.6A

Contents

Loyev Books

INTRODUCTION

Dialoguing with ancient philosophers

The topic of this book is ancient Western philosophy, but this is not an ordinary history book. Its main purpose is not to summarize what ancient philosophers have written, but to invite readers to "resonate" with the ideas of those philosophers in a personal and creative way.

By "resonating" with a philosophical text we mean engaging in a personal dialogue with it, somewhat like the dialogue between the saxophone and trumpet in an improvised jazz session. The two instruments do not discuss each other's music but rather play side by side, responding to each other, complementing each other, and creating a new musical piece together. Likewise, the readers of this book are invited to "play along" with ancient philosophers and create their own philosophical music.

Of course, in order to resonate with a given philosopher we must first understand what that philosopher has written. The saxophonist has to hear what the trumpet is playing in order to resonate with it appropriately. For this reason, each chapter of this book is composed of two parts: First, a brief exposition of a selected idea of the philosopher in question; and second, suggestions for ways to resonate with this idea.

When resonating with the ideas of ancient philosophers, we are in effect conversing on fundamental issues of life and reality, which is the main topic of philosophy. The history of philosophy contains a broad variety of approaches which have developed in complex ways throughout many centuries, but to the extent that they are philosophical, they all do something similar: they engage in a systematic discussion of general, fundamental issues of existence, and attempt to address them by constructing general theories about them.

In this book we will focus on selected thinkers from ancient philosophy. As commonly defined, ancient philosophy (in the West) includes the historical discourse that started in ancient Greece more than twenty-five centuries ago, around the 6th century BC, and lasted for more than a thousand years until the fall of the Roman empire and the rise of Christianity to dominance, around the fifth century AD. As we will see, the issues which these ancient thinkers explored are still relevant to us today.

This book is an interactive study of fourteen influential ancient philosophies, and a practical guide to contemplating on their deep insights. It regards ancient philosophies not merely as theories of the past, but as starting points for the reader's own personal exploration.

The contemplative exercises presented here have been developed in the international group-activity of *Deep Philosophy*, which is an approach to reflecting on philosophical life-issues from our inner depth.

To learn more about this approach, see the DPhilo website at: https://dphilo.org/

PART A

THE PRE-SOCRATIC PHILOSOPHERS

Western philosophy was born in the 6th century BC in the ancient Greek world. It was the first known systematic attempt in the West to understand the world in terms of general, universal principles, and to describe them in theories.

The first Greek philosophers developed theories about the natural world, about the laws that govern the universe, about human nature and ethical behavior. It took less than two centuries for the greatest ancient philosophers of Western history to appear on the scene: Socrates (5th century BC), his student Plato (5th-4th centuries BC), and Plato's student Aristotle (4th century BC). The influence of these three thinkers on later philosophy has been profound, and they can be seen as major pillars of Western thought. The thinkers who philosophized before them are commonly called the *Pre-Socratic philosophers*.

Many of the Pre-Socratic philosophers wrote books, but unfortunately, they have been lost to us. What remains today are only fragments, which are citations from later ancient philosophers who quoted them.

Chapter 1

THE MILESIANS – THEORIES

Introduction

The first known Western philosophers lived in the 6th century in the city of Miletus, located on the western shore of present-day Turkey. As far as we know, the first three Milesian thinkers were Thales, Anaximander and Anaximenes, and their innovation was a new intellectual agenda: to explain the natural world in terms of a small number of universal principles. Prior to them, it was common to understand natural phenomena in terms of gods, spirits, or other supernatural beings who presumably controlled events in the world according to their will. Why, for example, do we have rain on earth? A pre-philosophical mind might reply that the rain-god wants plants to grow and animals to flourish. In contrast, the idea of general, impersonal principles that apply universally to everything was revolutionary.

The Milesian thinkers were especially interested in the composition of the natural world, and they used various considerations to determine the basic stuff of which everything is made: Everything is made of water (Thales), of an indefinite substance (Anaximander), or of air (Anaximenes).

We know today that these early theories are incorrect (sand, for example, is not made of water), and yet they represent a new way of thinking. In several respects, these early philosophers took a crucial step towards philosophical-scientific thought: They developed universal theories about the world; they distinguished between the way the world appears and its hidden underlying structure; they explained all phenomena in terms of a small number of basic principles; they proposed that all matter is made of fundamental building blocks; and they recognized the power of reason in developing a systematic understanding of reality.

Reflecting: How can we understand our world?

Let us focus our encounter with the first philosophers on the notion of *understanding*. This is an important topic in our lives – we all seek to understand ourselves and our world, and it also concerned the first philosophers.

Imagine that we live somewhere in the Mediterranean region 2700 years ago, just before the birth of Western philosophy. As thoughtful and sensitive people, we marvel at the richness of the world around us, its myriad creatures and objects, its many shapes and colors and sounds in innumerable variations. We wonder: How should we relate to this cosmic marvel?

Several options stand before us. We could, for example, celebrate nature in dance and music. Or, we could conclude that some divine power must be behind natural events and pray to it for protection. Or, we could draw artistic inspiration from the beauty of nature and compose beautiful poems and paintings. We could also meditate in silence and be one with the universe.

But the first Western philosophers, twenty-six centuries ago, chose a different, intellectual approach. What they wanted was not just to celebrate or manipulate hidden powers, but primarily to understand – not only to understand this or that detail, but to understand nature as a whole. Take a step back, they tell us, and think carefully and objectively: Why is the world the way it is?

And if we heed them, we will find ourselves in the realm of rational explanation.

But what kind of rational explanation could satisfy our search for an understanding of the natural world? Should we understand it as a product of the will of the gods? Or as a battleground of the struggle between the powers of good and the powers of evil? Or as a cosmic organism that grows and develops through history towards some goal – perfection for instance?

The Milesians' response: Theories

The first Western philosophers chose a different alternative: Forget about myths and legends, and let us understand the world in terms of universal principles. These will be objective laws that apply to everything, leaving no room for the personal whim of supernatural powers.

And now we are in the realm of philosophical-scientific understanding. Using objective principles, we can construct a general theory about nature. Thales, for example, the first philosopher, theorized that everything is made of water. Water, he thought, is the basic substance that is transformed from ice into liquid water and from water into steam – and by extension, can be transformed into anything else in nature. Anaximander offered a different theory. He apparently reasoned that the basic stuff of the world cannot be a specific visible material such as water, but must be an indefinite substance that has no specific quality. The third philosopher, Anaximenes, theorized that everything is made of air, perhaps because air gives life to the living beings who breathe it.

We are now thinking in terms of philosophical theories of reality. Many centuries later, after the birth of modern science, we will hear that everything is made of atoms or electrons or quarks – but in many respects the basic idea will remain the same.

Some *key concepts* to reflect upon:

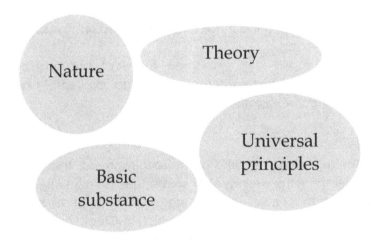

Contemplating

After this brief glimpse at the ideas of the Milesian thinkers, let us start a personal dialogue with them. This means that our focus will now shift from seeking to learn what they said to seeking to develop our own insights in response to theirs.

For this purpose, we will contemplate. By "contemplating" we mean thinking deeply within ourselves in search of new insights, as opposed to intellectualizing in the abstract and imposing our ready-made opinions. In contemplative thinking we listen inwardly and let ideas surface in our mind. The result can be rich new understandings, often accompanied by a sense of marvel, of inner silence, and of preciousness.

Contemplation is somewhat similar to meditation in that it requires you to attain a special attentive state of mind. But unlike many forms of meditation, the purpose of contemplation is not inner silence for its own sake, but a deep understanding of ideas. The contemplative state of mind is not easy to achieve. Our mind's automatic tendency is to analyze and judge and express opinions, and it takes practice to push aside these tendencies and open a space of inner listening.

Here we will conduct three forms of philosophical contemplation: *text-contemplation*, *visual contemplation*, and *issue-contemplation*.

1. *Text-contemplation*

The following are some of the few fragments that have survived from the writings of Anaximander. Here he offers his ambitious theory: Everything in nature is made of the same basic stuff, namely the *Apeiron*, which in Greek means the non-limited or the indefinite. It is an indefinite stuff in the sense that it is neither blue nor yellow, neither hard nor soft, neither heavy nor light, but rather devoid of any quality.

While reading these fragments, let us reflect on the idea – so widely accepted today but so innovative back then – that theoretical thinking can offer us access to the hidden structure of the world. Theories can portray the world very differently from the way it appears to our senses. Consider the familiar things you see around you – trees and stones and chairs and houses, as well as your friends' bodies and your own body – and try to imagine them as clumps of indeterminate stuff as Anaximander tells us, or perhaps as clusters of miniscule atoms as modern scientific theories tells us. The world is no longer what you assumed it was!

What does this kind of theoretical thinking do to you? How does it change your attitude to the world around you, to yourself and to others?

Contemplate on these issues as you read Anaximander's text silently and slowly, savoring the words and the images and letting them speak in your mind. You may want to read the text in this manner several times over and over again and note the flow of ideas within you.[1]

1. *The Non-Limited is the origin of all things. ... It is the source from which things arise and into which they return once more when they pass away, as is determined by necessity; for they make reparation and satisfaction to one another for their injustice [=imbalance] according to the appointed time.*

2. *This [the Non-Limited] is eternal and ageless, and it encompasses all the worlds.*

2. *Visual contemplation*

To enrich your contemplation, you may use the drawing that appears in this chapter. Like all the drawings in this book, it was designed especially for visual contemplation. While keeping in mind the Milesians' ideas, examine the different elements in the drawing. Let your eyes glide over them gently and slowly, stopping every once in a while on a specific detail, inspecting it and letting it trigger insights in your mind. Don't try to impose on the image your own interpretation; let it speak within you.

3. *Issue-contemplation*

Just as we can contemplate on a text or on a drawing, we can also contemplate on a philosophical issue. The challenge is to do so not as an intellectual exercise, but as a personal dialogue. Let us push aside our automatic tendency to analyze and express opinions, and instead listen inwardly to the following issue as it "speaks" in us:

Theories are a great tool. They unify the world for us, they tell us in advance what to expect, they allow us to build machines and control our environment. But can they be applied to everything? Theories seem to work well for understanding inanimate objects such as stones and clouds, but can they also apply to myself? Can a theory add to my understanding of my own experience of love, or of hope, or anxiety?

Indeed, when we theorize about a personal situation and analyze it, we are sometimes left with the uncomfortable feeling that something has been left out. Somehow, we feel, the theory fails to do justice to that which is unique, vague, subjective, fundamentally personal. Is it possible that theoretical thinking is not suitable for understanding our own life, especially our personal experience? And if so, why?

Seeds of contemplation

To contemplate on this philosophical issue, it may help to use a "seed of contemplation" – a concept or metaphor that would serve as a starting point for a deeper reflection. Here are several suggestions for such starting points. Choose one of them (or compose your own) and let it grow and unfold in your mind.

a) The metaphor of **looking from the inside versus from the outside**: When I theorize about my experiences, I inspect them "from the outside" so to speak, observing them as if they were somebody else's. In contrast, when I sense my experience without yet thinking, I sense them "from the inside," from my own perspective. This difference in perspective might be why theorizing seems to miss something about my inner life.

b) The concept of **uniqueness**: A theory always uses generalizations, and a generalization applies to items that are repeatable, in other words that occur again and again. But perhaps some personal experiences are unique and unrepeatable, so that they escape theoretical generalizations.

c) The metaphor of **before words**: When we theorize, we think in words. But sometimes we encounter reality directly,

before our mind starts thinking in words: I relate to you
through love, I understand the natural landscape through
the sense of beauty, I feel the divine through a sense of awe.
At such moments, words and theories fall silent.

Chapter 2

HERACLITUS – ALL IS IN FLUX

Introduction

Heraclitus lived around the year 500 BC in the Greek city of Ephesus in Asia Minor, in present-day Turkey. Little is known about his life, but later ancient historians wrote that he was from an influential family, that he was a snob and wrote in a difficult language so that only few would understand him (hence the name "Heraclitus the obscure"), and that he was a pessimist (hence the name "the weeping philosopher"). He died of some illness at the age of 60.

Heraclitus wrote one book in which he attempted to cover all knowledge. Only several fragments from the book remain today, and their main themes are: that there is a universal law that governs everything – the Logos; that most people are half-asleep and do not understand the Logos; that everything in the world is in constant change; that fire is the basic principle of reality; that good and bad are relative to one's perspective; and that natural processes have the form of a conflict between opposites that combine into harmony.

Reflecting: Is the world things or changes?

Imagine that you are at a party in somebody's house. You step out for a breath of fresh air and return ten minutes later. At a first glance, nothing seems to have changed – the "same" people, the "same" room and furniture, the "same" clothes and jewelry. Your mind sees sameness in everything, automatically and unthinkingly.

But when you look more closely, you notice that numerous changes have occurred. The man in the corner, who was grumpy before, is smiling now, and he has taken off his sweater. The tall young woman is no longer sitting silently by herself, but is standing and talking animatedly with somebody. The newspaper on the table is now open and torn a little. The red rug is crumpled at the corner. The light is somewhat different, perhaps because the sun had come out from behind the clouds, and the room is brighter than it was ten minutes ago.

We are so used to changes that we hardly notice them. Our mind assumes that things are "the same" as before. But, asks Heraclitus, what if there are no stable "things" around you, only changes – a continuous stream of changes like a flowing river with its myriad ripples and eddies?

And Heraclitus adds a second reason to shed doubt on the idea of fixed things: Things are not straightforwardly what they are, since each thing contains its opposite. The woman's serious facial expression is also comical. The big man seems tiny next to the huge sculpture. The electric wire that goes from the wall to the lamp also goes from the lamp to the wall.

And a third consideration: Conflict and harmony are not as alien to each other as you might think. If you listen to the young couple singing by the piano, you will note that although the woman's soprano is very different from the man's tenor, nevertheless the two voices join together into a harmonious song. Likewise, the fierce competition between the two ping-pong players on the porch is beautiful to the point of perfection. And the vocal political argument at the center of the room is part of a friendship.

So what is reality? Is it made of stable and distinct things that only change appearance and location, or is it a world of changes and harmonious oppositions? Are the fundamental building blocks that compose reality things or transformations?

Heraclitus' response: All is in flux

Heraclitus responds: Once you resist your automatic tendency to see sameness and instead pay attention to the changes, you will realize that everything is in flux. Fixed things are a mere appearance. The world, like fire, is ever-changing. Indeed, if you think that a tree is a stable thing, then fast forward a video of that tree and you will see a process of growth and decay.

Nevertheless, Heraclitus notes, our world is not in chaos. Although everything keeps changing, it does not do so arbitrarily. Your table does not suddenly fly in the air or turn into an elephant.

The flow of changes is ruled by patterns, by rules, or as Heraclitus puts it, by the "Logos" that keeps the flow within limits. Logos is the way of the flux, indeed of the cosmic drama.

Some *key concepts* to reflect upon:

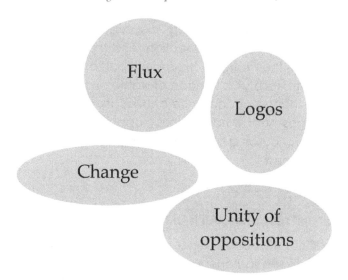

Contemplating

Now that we understand the basics of Heraclitus' vision, let us turn to contemplation – in other words, quietly thinking from our inner depth. Instead of analyzing his ideas on the intellectual level, we want to open ourselves to personal insights that might surface in our minds in response. We want, in other words, to "resonate" with his view.

1. Text-contemplation

Heraclitus' book is now lost, but some later quotations by later ancient writers have survived. To contemplate on the following selection, you might want to first center yourself for a few moments with eyes closed, and then read the words slowly and gently, letting them speak within you. You might also try a recitation exercise: Select a sentence that seems to you pregnant with meaning, and keep reading it slowly again and again. Listen to the sound of the sentence as it resonates in you and try to discern insights that might appear in your mind.[2]

2. *Although the Law of Reason (Logos) is common to all, the majority of people live as though they had an understanding of their own.*

8. *Things which are unlike are joined together, and differences result in the most beautiful harmony, and all things take place through strife.*

30. *This world, which is the same for all, was not made by any god or man, but it always was, and is, and shall be, an ever living fire, kindled in due measure and extinguished in due measure.*

41. *There is one wisdom: to understand the intelligence through which all things are governed through all things.*

51. *The harmony of the world is a harmony of oppositions, as in the case of the bow and of the lyre.*

60. *The way upward and downward are one and the same.*

91. *Into the same river you could not step twice, because other waters keep flowing.*

126. *Cold becomes warm, and warm cold; wet becomes dry, and dry wet.*

2. *Visual contemplation*

Visual contemplation allows us to delve into a philosopher's ideas in a non-verbal way. In this chapter, like in all the chapters of this book, you will find a drawing. Inspect it silently while keeping Heraclitus' ideas in your mind. Let your eyes hover over it gently and freely, occasionally stopping to examine some detail. Given enough time and inner silence, the image might trigger new understandings in your mind.

3. *Issue-contemplation*

Consider Heraclitus' view that everything keeps changing. This presumably applies to my everyday life too, to my moods, my body, my friends and colleagues, my house – they all change from day to day and from moment to moment. Most people do not notice it, Heraclitus tells us, because they notice just the misleading surface of stability and sameness. Only the wise recognize the constant flux, the transformation of opposites, and the Logos that governs them.

This raises the following issue for contemplation: If I were to become one of those wise people who are fully aware of the cosmic flux, how would I live my life? How would I have to change myself in order to deal with the continuous changes around me and in me? Indeed, what is wisdom in a world that seems to offer nothing stable, no ground to stand on, no fixed facts to grasp?

Seeds of contemplation

To contemplate on the meaning of wisdom in a world of change, we could start with a seed of contemplation – a metaphor or concept to orient our contemplation. Here are several suggestions:

a) The metaphor of **flowing water**: As a wise person I am helped by a guiding awareness – that I am not a "thing" but a small current in the cosmic flow. Like such a current, everything in me keeps changing, and I accept my situation. I don't try to hold on to anything stable, I don't resist changing. I am water, and I know the ways of water. I know the Logos of change from my inner experience.

b) The metaphor of a **ship captain**: A wise captain knows the Logos of the sea and how to use it for his purpose. He knows how to go with the wind or against it, how to navigate in a storm and how to drop anchor. He can anticipate the coming tide or squall, and prepare in advance.

c) The concept of **marvel**: In an ever-changing world, I possess no fixed knowledge; I can only marvel. I marvel at the restless "fire" of the universe that keeps dancing and transforming, and at the Logos that gives its flames ever-changing shapes and colors. Every moment is new and lively, and I savor its freshness.

Chapter 3

P ARMENIDES – BEING IS ONE

Introduction

Parmenides of Elea was a Greek philosopher who lived around the end of the 5th century B.C. and the beginning of the 4th. His influence on Western philosophy has been considerable. He wrote a philosophical poem, large fragments of which survived, describing his imaginary journey to the sacred temple of some unnamed goddess. There, the goddess explains to him two ways of thinking: The way of common opinion, which is based on sensory perception, and the way of truth, which is based on reason (logos). While the way of common opinion portrays the world as a plurality of things which move and change and are created and destroyed, the way of truth shows that this is impossible. Movement, change, and creation mean a negation of being (it was here but now it is not, it is this but not that, it is now but was not earlier), which is not possible. What is – is; and what is not – is not. Thus, being just is, without division or change.

Reflecting: What is Being?

Sometimes you experience a sense of wonder: What is this reality which I always find encompassing me, which includes me and everything that is?

It may be tempting to reply dismissively: Reality is simply everything taken together, the sum of every thing that exists: stones and flowers and rivers and stars.

But no, the ancient philosopher Parmenides would respond, that is not what I am asking. I am not wondering about the existence of individual things, but about existence in general. The tree is, the stone is, the mountain is – but what is this is-ness? What does it mean for something to be? In short, what is Being?

That is, Parmenides tells us, what the wonder is about: The surprise that something is, the is-ness of everything.

Parmenides' response: What is just is

Being, or is-ness, Parmenides explains, cannot be a particular quality or thing. It cannot be green as opposed to blue, or hard as opposed to soft, because it encompasses everything that is, whether green or blue or yellow, whether soft or hard. Being is – it cannot contain anything that "is not" – so it cannot be one thing but "not" another. It must lie beyond all particular qualities and all individual things, beyond all distinctions and differences. It is not limited by any boundary or qualification. It is pure is-ness.

Likewise, Being cannot change or move. It cannot be at one moment here, and "not" here at the next moment. Being just is. And what is not, cannot possibly be part of it.

But this leads us to a surprising conclusion: It means that reality is not composed of a multiplicity of things, as we normally assume. When I look around, I seem to perceive many things – trees and tables and birds and clouds – but in fact they are all one Being. Evidently, our senses mislead us. We must trust only our reason.

Parmenides' vision might seem strange, because it denies that reality is made of many things, as it appears to our senses. Let us try to get an intuitive sense of what he is saying.

Normally I note particular things. I look at this thing or that thing, I touch this or that, I manipulate this object or that object. Even I myself seem to be an object among objects, and I encounter other humans as one object encounters another. Yet, in special moments something different happens to me. My attention detaches itself from specific objects and I no longer grasp this thing or that thing. I am open to the entire universe, to reality as a whole, to everything that is. Being itself manifests itself to me.

And now I note: Beyond the specific colors and the particular shapes, beyond the many details around me and in me, I witness the pure is-ness that underlies all, the all-encompassing Being. And then there is awe and wonder. All I can say is: What is, is.

Some *key concepts* to reflect upon:

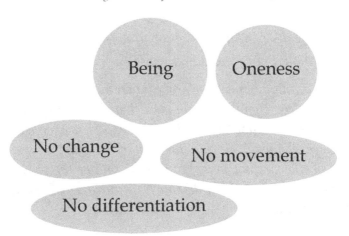

Contemplating

Now that we understand what seems to be the logic of Parmenides' vision, let us try to relate to it more deeply and personally. Our purpose is not just to understand it as an abstract theory, but to sense it from the inside and discern its personal implications. Let us, in short, contemplate on his vision.

1. Text-contemplation

Read Parmenides' words very slowly, savor the words and ideas, and let them arouse in you wonder and marvel. Let them speak within you. What are they telling you about yourself and your world? In particular, can you recall or imagine having experienced a sense of pure existence, perhaps of "I exist" or "Everything exists"? Have you ever had the experience of the realness of reality, the is-ness that unifies everything? And if so, what does this experience tell you about what it means to exist?

Here are relevant excerpts from Parmenides' philosophical poem:[3]

> **3.** It is the same thing to think or to be. [An alternative translation: Being and thinking are one and the same.]
>
> **7.** For this can never be proved: that the things that are not, are. You should restrain your thought from this way of inquiry, and not let your habitual experience force you to go in this way, which is the way of the wandering eye and of the ear that is full of sounds and of the tongue. Rather, judge by reason the much-disputed proof which I here explain.

8. *One path only is left for us to speak about, namely, that what is, is. In it there are very many signs showing that being is uncreated and indestructible. Because it is complete, immovable, and without end. Nor was it ever, nor will it be, for it is now, all at once, a continuous whole. For what kind of origin for it will you look for? In what way and from what source could it have grown?*

2. Visual contemplation

Let us now relate to Parmenides' vision with the help of the drawing you will find in this chapter. Images have the power to trigger in us understandings that are less conceptual and more intuitive and holistic.

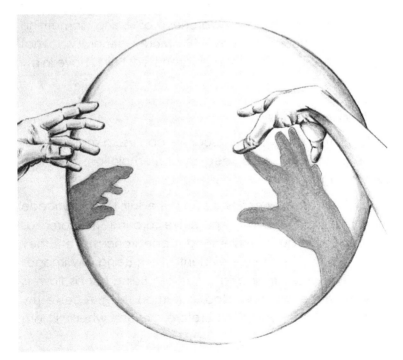

Let your eyes wander gently over the drawing and listen inwardly to insights that may arise in your mind. As opposed to previous drawings, this one contains few details. The reason is clear: In Parmenides' world there is only one uniform being without distinctions or change. Let us contemplate on this oneness.

3. Issue-contemplation

The awareness of the is-ness that underlies everything is a special state of mind that seems marvelous, but it is short-lived. If I happen to experience it, then sooner or later it is bound to dissolve, leaving me again in my ordinary affairs and states of mind. Most likely I will find myself working or chatting or arguing or watching TV, and forget all about the experience.

Should I be disappointed that I lost so quickly the sense of Being? Indeed, is the awareness of Being something valuable? Should I seek it? More generally, what significance, if any, does the awareness of Being have in my life?

Seeds of contemplation

To contemplate on this issue, we can use a metaphor or concept to serve as a seed of contemplation. Here are several suggestions:

a) The metaphor of **flowers from the soil**: I may concede that the many things I perceive around me are, as Parmenides argues, misleading appearances. Yet, they come from somewhere – evidently from Being. My images of reality receive their existence from Being just as flowers grow from the soil. And I too, a human thing, receive my existence from Being. Therefore, even when I am preoccupied with images of plurality, I can still sense through them the power of Being that is at their root.

b) The concept of *accepting my limitations*: If Being is the true reality, then I yearn to connect to it forever. But this is impossible for me, because I am not an enlightened sage or an angel in heaven; I am just an ordinary, limited human being. So if once in a while I get a glimpse of the essence that hides underneath the surface, what more can I ask for? How fortunate I am – to be a creature who is lost in petty affairs, yet to be granted sometimes, in special moments, a vision of ultimate Being.

c) The metaphor of *two lives*: When I am absorbed in everyday matters, only one part of me is involved. In another dimension of myself I am with a greater reality, with Being. But this means that I live two different lives in parallel: a life of plurality and a life of one unitary Being. And so, even when I am lost in trivialities in one life, in my other life I am still taking part in reality itself.

Chapter 4

E MPEDOCLES – LOVE VERSUS STRIFE

Introduction

Empedocles was born in the early 5th century BC in the Greek city of Acragas in Sicily. On the basis of later records it appears that he was born to an aristocratic family, that he was a successful speaker, practiced medicine, and was involved in political activity. He died at the age of sixty, according to a legend by jumping into the mouth of the volcano Aetna.

Empedocles composed at least two philosophical poems, "On nature" and "On purifications." In the former poem, parts of which survived, he explains the structure of matter in terms of four "roots" and two forces. The roots of matter are fire, earth, air and water, of which every material thing is composed in different proportions. They are indestructible and eternal, and are governed by two forces that keep them balanced through periodic or local increase and decrease.

These two forces are Love and Strife, the power of attraction and unity versus the power of repulsion and separation. Since they change periodically in intensity, the cosmos undergoes cycles in which either Love or Strife reigns, the first resulting in periods of unity while the second in periods of destruction.

Reflecting: Which basic forces govern our world?

If you live in the fifth century BC and try to understand the basic forces of nature, you do not have the benefit of modern science to guide you. The modern ideas of conducting controlled experiments in the laboratory, of measuring your results mathematically, building theoretical models and testing them in the lab – all these are still many centuries away. You have to rely on your everyday observations and your reasoning.

Now, if you were a thinker of the fifth century BC trying to determine the basic forces that govern everything that exists in nature, you would probably be baffled by the wondrous variety of observable phenomena: hard stationary objects such as stones, water that flows, fire that dances in the stove, plants that grow slowly and produce fruit and flowers, animals that walk and give birth and make noises, human beings who converse and work and fight and play. Each of these displays a confusing range of behaviors under different circumstances. From this perspective, how would you characterize the basic forces that control all the activities in the cosmos?

Empedocles' response: Love and Strife

At a first glance, the visible world around us is so rich and diverse that it is difficult to see any common process that characterizes all of it. What can possibly be common to a cloud floating in the sky, a plant producing a flower, an earthquake, and a human being writing a letter? It may seem that each thing has its own principles of action.

Yet, Empedocles sees commonalities in this confusing variety. He suggests that all natural phenomena can be understood in terms of different degrees of harmony or unity versus conflict or separation. On the one hand we see two dogs fighting, an earthquake that devastates a city, or a sickness that destroys the body – all these contain conflict, disturbance of unity, fragmentation and separation. On the other hand we notice a wonderful equilibrium between the plants and animals of a forest, the togetherness between two good friends, or the coordination among members of a peaceful community.

Thus, suggests Empedocles, the world and life can be seen as governed by two opposing forces, that of Love – the power of unity, and that of Strife – the power or conflict and separation. These two basic forces oppose each other in the universe, so that sometimes the one has the upper hand and sometimes the other.

Some *key concepts* to reflect upon:

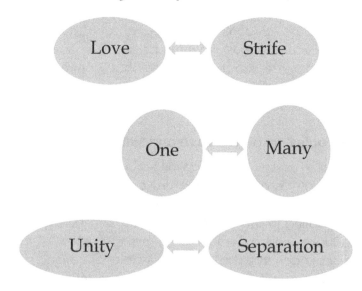

Contemplating

Empedocles' view of the forces of Love and of Strife was intended as a general theory of the world, but we are entitled to ask ourselves how it applies, more specifically, to our own personal lives. To what extent can we understand our lives as characterized by those two forces? And even more specifically, to what extent does the idea of this opposition shed light on our personal experience?

When we look at life through the lens of new concepts, we often discover new perspectives and reach new understandings. Let us then contemplate on life – our personal life and life in general – through the lens of Empedocles' opposing forces of Love and Strife.

1. *Text-contemplation*

Let us start by contemplating on some relevant fragments that have survived from Empedocles' writings. Read the text below slowly and silently, and ask yourself what it tells you about life. These two passages are from Empedocles' book *On Nature*:[4]

> **17.** *I will tell of a twofold truth: At one time the One is united from the Many, at another time the One separates to become Many. Twofold is the birth of things, twofold is their death: At one time the union of the Many results in birth and then death; at another time, whatever grew before separates and dies.*
>
> *And this long interchange will never end. Sometimes the elements unite through Love and become One, while at other times they separate again through the hate of Strife.*

And in so far as the One is able to grow from the Many, and the Many grow from the scattering of the One, they keep being born in time and are not stable. And in so far as the long interchange never ends, they remain unchanged as they move through the cyclic process of the world.

21. Observe the sun, warm and everywhere bright. Observe the eternal stars, always steeped in liquid heat and glowing radiance. See also the rain, obscure and cold and dark, and how from the earth emerge what is green and firm. And in periods of anger they are divided into many different shapes, while in Love they come together and yearn for each other.

Because from these [basic four] elements grow all that was, or is, or will ever be – all trees, and men and women, beasts and birds, and fish nourished in deep waters, and even the long-lived gods who are excellent in honor. Because these [elements] are all that exist, and, as they run through one another they receive new faces, they change through varied mixing.

2. Visual contemplation

Keeping in mind Empedocles' idea of Love and Strife as two universal principles, examine gently the drawing in this chapter and let it speak within you. What does it tell you about the nature of those two forces?

3. *Issue-contemplation*

Consider the dynamics, suggested by Empedocles, of Love and unity versus Strife and fragmentation. These two forces intensify and weaken through time, so that in some periods love dominates, while in other periods strife rules.

To some extent, we all experience those forces acting within us: On the one hand we are familiar with anger, hate, jealousy, inner conflict, self-doubt, as well as competition, individualism, the urge to be left alone, all of which work to fragment the whole into parts: me versus others, one feeling versus another. On the other hand, we are also familiar with the experiences of empathy, friendship, attraction, mutual understanding, a sense of harmony and wholeness.

How can I handle these opposing forces and navigate my life towards my personal goals? Am I able to influence them and tame them to suit my purposes? More generally, how should I live my life in the midst of their activity?

Seeds of contemplation

Here are some seeds which might help us contemplate on this issue:

a) The metaphor of **the gardener**: I cannot completely control the forces that act within and around me. I cannot erase all my angers, nor create love in my heart. I can only try to cultivate or suppress them, and my success is bound to be partial. But to the extent possible, I will work to make my "garden" whole and beautiful. I will use the forces of strife to separate myself from what threatens the perfection of my "garden," and I will use the forces of love to connect to what contributes to it.

b) The concept of **the king**: With enough will-power, I can learn to control many of my urges and emotions. And to the extent that I can do so, I will act as the king of my private kingdom and care for its proper functioning. A kingdom cannot be based on love only – it needs policing and defense forces on the one hand, and cooperation on the other hand. Likewise, the well-being of my personal "kingdom" requires both love and strife, and it is my task as a ruler to make sure that each of them acts optimally in the appropriate circumstances.

c) The concept of **world-harmony**: As an individual person amongst millions of others, I have a negligible influence on the state of the world. Even my influence on my own psychology is limited. But to the extent possible, I will work to nurture the love in me, and thus contribute my tiny part to the harmony of the world in which we all live.

Chapter 5

ANAXAGORAS – THE COSMIC MIND

Introduction

Anaxagoras was born at around 500 BC in the Greek city of Clazomenae in today's Turkey, which was at that time under the control of the Persian empire. As a young man he came to Athens, where he lived for more than twenty years until he was forced to leave, probably because of his association with the Athenian leader Pericles.

For Anaxagoras, everything in the world is made of tiny indestructible elements, or "seeds," which are of many different kinds and are mixed with each other throughout the universe. In addition, he also posits a power – Mind, or Nous in Greek, which puts the world in motion. This influences the concentration of seeds in different places and thus separates them into objects of various kinds such as stones and trees, each with its own composition and characteristics.

Reflecting: Why is the world organized?

Anaxagoras, like Parmenides before him, accepts that something that exists cannot turn into nothing and cannot be born out of nothing. Therefore, the basic stuff of which the world is made is fixed and unchanging. The changes that we seem to see around us – trees growing and getting old, houses being erected or torn down, clouds moving, etc. – are only rearrangements of fixed elements. These elements, which he calls "seeds," are infinitely small, eternal and unchanging. The material objects that we find in the world are clusters of seeds of every kind, so that each kind of seed is present in every object – but in different proportions. To give an example (which is not Anaxagoras'), a stone is hard because it is made mostly of hard seeds and only few soft seeds, while wool is made primarily of soft seeds. And when it burns to ashes, its seeds do not disappear but get mixed up with other seeds in the environment.

One might expect that the seeds that compose the universe would completely mix with each other, so that the world would be like an undifferentiated mixture. Yet, what we see around us is a highly organized world, made of distinct objects: stones, plants, animals, people, houses, and so on. Furthermore, each kind of object displays a specific kind of behavior: Trees grow in the ground and do not fly in the air, and they grow leaves but not hands. A tree remains a tree, and it follows the typical life-cycle of a tree. Mountains do not melt into gold, and people do not grow wings. Despite occasional surprises, world-events and life-events are not in a state of chaos, but follow more or less familiar patterns.

How can we explain the organization of the world? What kind of forces are responsible for maintaining order in the world?

Anaxagoras' response: The cosmic Mind

At a first glance, two alternative responses seem appealing: One possibility is that the world is guided by some god who imposes order upon the seeds that compose the world, aggregating them into definite objects and making sure that each of them follows its proper behavior. Alternatively, one might argue that the world is not guided by anybody, and the apparent organization of the world is a result of blind forces that act upon the seeds. Blind mechanical forces create order by themselves.

Anaxagoras rejects both alternatives and takes a middle path. On the one hand, he seems to reason, arbitrary mechanical forces are not sufficient to ensure that the world would be organized. Without an organizing power, the seeds that make up the world would be mixed with each other into a uniform blend, rather than separate objects.

On the other hand, the organizing power is not a god with a personality and a personal will. There is no reason to assume that it is a "somebody" who thinks and acts intentionally, and who imposes on the world some preconceived purpose. Indeed, Plato and Aristotle were disappointed with Anaxagoras' theory because it denied that the universe has a moral world-order.

Anaxagoras calls this force "Nous," which in Greek means Mind. This cosmic Mind causes the seeds of the world to aggregate into separate objects with specific qualities that follow specific patterns of behavior. It thus organizes the world into an intelligible whole.

Some *key concepts* to reflect upon:

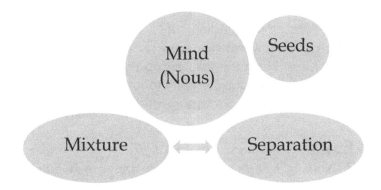

Contemplating

Only fragments from Anaxagoras' book remain today, but it seems that he was mainly interested in explaining the natural world, and less interested in human life and psychology. Nevertheless, in order to bring our contemplation closer to life, we can expand his theory to also include human lives. This expanded theory would say that our personal lives too follow an intelligible order created by the Mind's action. That is why we can discern in a person's life specific stages, processes, developments, and why we can say intelligent things about them. Life is governed by an intelligible order, an idea that would appear again and again throughout the history of philosophy and of science in many different variations.

What is the intelligible order that characterizes life and the world? And on a personal level, what is the intelligible order that characterizes your personal life?

Anaxagoras' answer, in terms of Nous, is enigmatic. What does it mean that a cosmic Mind maintains order and organization in our world and life?

1. Text-contemplation

To address this question, let us contemplate on Anaxagoras' own words, focusing on those sections that deal with Nous. Read the following passages slowly, savor the words and the images, and try to discern what they tell you about how Nous shapes your world.[5]

> **12.** All other things contain a portion of everything, while Nous is infinite and self-ruling, and is mixed with nothing, but is alone by itself. Because if it was not by itself, but was mixed with anything else, it would have a share of all things, if it was mixed with anything. Because in everything there is a portion of everything, as I have said before. And the things mixed with it would prevent it from having over anything the power it now has when it is alone by itself. Because it is the thinnest of all things and the purest, and it has all knowledge about everything, and has the greatest power. Nous has power over all things that have life, both greater and smaller.
>
> ... And all the things that are mingled together and separated and distinguished from each other are all known by Nous. And Nous set in order all the things that would be, and those that were and are not now, and those that are now.

2. Visual contemplation

While keeping in mind Anaxagoras' vision, examine quietly the drawing in this chapter. Notice any insight or image that appears in your mind, and try to articulate what it tells you about the nature of the cosmic Nous.

3. *Issue-contemplation*

If a cosmic Mind exists, then how does it relate to me and my individual mind? And how should I relate to it? More generally, how does the existence of the cosmic Mind affect my life and my individual mind?

Seeds of contemplation

The following are suggested seeds to enrich our contemplation on these issues:

a) The metaphor of *a mind inside a mind:* I am not an isolated mind, because my mind is contained in a bigger, cosmic Mind. Just as my human mind contains thoughts and experiences, likewise the cosmic Mind must contain all the ideas and experiences in the cosmos, including my own. In this sense, my mind is a small part of the cosmic Mind. And although I know that this part is very small, still I am inspired by the knowledge that I am part of a vast Mind.

b) The concept of *visibility:* If the cosmos has a Mind that encompasses everything in the world including me, then it knows me completely. It knows each of my thoughts and experiences, my hopes and fears and intentions. Therefore, I am completely visible to the cosmic Mind, and there is nothing I can hide from it. In the face of the all-knowing Mind, I have no privacy, no secret, no hiding place. I feel utterly naked to the Mind's understanding.

c) The concept of *my intelligible life*: If the cosmic Mind controls everything that happens in my life, then I should be relieved to know that my life is intelligible, even if I myself cannot understand how. What appears to be arbitrary or meaningless in my life is in truth not so. And although I may not understand the meaning of my life, I can trust that my life is not in vain.

Chapter 6

Democritus – All Is Atoms

Introduction

Democritus (about 460–370 BC) was a Greek philosopher who lived in the city of Abdera, in present-day Greece. He is best known today for his theory of atoms, reminiscent of modern atomic theory (although its details are quite different).

According to some sources, Democritus received the theory of atoms from his teacher Leucippus, about whom very little is known. It is therefore impossible to determine today which parts of Democritus' atomic theory are originally his, and which parts came from his teacher. In any case, Democritus' theory posits that the world is made of "atoms" that are indivisible particles, solid, unchangeable and indestructible, and that move in the void.

It is possible that this theory was a reaction to Parmenides, who had argued that Being cannot turn into non-being, or be created out of non-being (nothingness). Democritus' atomic theory agrees that the basic units of reality, or atoms, are unchangeable and can never turn into nothingness. Yet, in contrast to Parmenides' theory, it also explains how motion and change are possible – in terms of different arrangements of atoms.

Reflecting: Is the whole just a collection of parts?

When we look around, we see material objects such as trees and rocks, chairs and houses. Even though each of these objects may appear as one whole unit, we know that it is made of smaller parts. A house, for example, is made of walls, windows, doors and a roof. And each of these parts can be broken down into smaller parts, which are themselves divisible into even smaller parts. How small are the smallest parts?

Democritus came to the conclusion that everything in nature is made of tiny basic particles. He conceived them as solid and indivisible "atoms" (meaning indivisibles in Greek) that move in the void. We don't know the precise considerations that led him to this view, since most of his writings have been lost. But it is worth noting that other philosophers of the 5th century BC, such as Empedocles and Anaxagoras, also proposed that material objects are made of small basic elements, although of different kinds. Modern scientific theories too view material objects as composed of microscopic particles – molecules, atoms, quarks – albeit on the basis of scientific evidence that was not available to Democritus.

The idea that material objects are made of particles may not seem surprising, since we know from experience that familiar objects can be broken into pieces. But so far we have been discussing inanimate objects. Can the same apply to animals, human beings, and even I myself?

Specifically, is it possible that my own thought, or my headache, my love or fear is also composed of tiny invisible particles moving in the void? Indeed, is it possible that I am not a unitary self as I experience myself to be, but a collection of multiple elements?

Democritus' response: I too am made of atoms

Democritus contends that everything in nature is composed of atoms, and this includes human beings, their thoughts, feelings, and experiences. Although very few fragments from his writings remain today, several later thinkers from antiquity explained his theory in some greater detail.

According to them, Democritus believed that perceptual qualities such as color or taste are mere "conventions" – in other words, artificial human views that do not reflect reality. When we look at an object, our perceptions are blind to the atoms of which it is made, and that's why we perceive it as one unitary thing with certain qualities such as color or texture.

Furthermore, not only the things we perceive, but also the perceptual act itself can be explained in terms of atoms. In visual perception, for example, images made of a thin layer of atoms fly from the surface of objects into the eyes. Likewise, taste is the result of atoms of different kinds impacting our tongues in different manners. Other mental states and experiences, such as thinking, can also be explained in terms of atoms and their movement. Finally, even the souls of living beings are made of atoms.

The details of Democritus' theories should not concern us here. From the perspective of modern science they are incorrect. The general point, however, is important: That not just material objects outside us, but also we and our states of mind are composed of invisible moving particles.

*Some **key concepts** to reflect upon:*

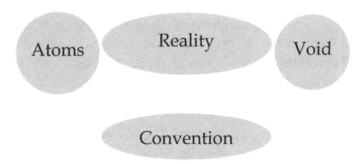

Contemplating

Democritus' view seems to contradict the way we experience ourselves. I normally experience myself as one, a unity, a single person – not as a cluster of separate elements moving about. Furthermore, each of my experiences feels to me as being one. My pain is one unitary feeling, not a collection of moving particles; and the same applies to my itch, my fear, my hope, my sensation of noise – each of these seems to be a unified whole.

Democritus (perhaps like some modern scientists) tells us that this is an illusion, and that I am in fact not unitary as I seem to be, but rather composed of atoms just like everything else in the universe. But is it really possible that I am so radically mistaken about myself? I who experience myself from the inside, from the most intimate perspective possible, can I possibly be living under an illusion about the kind of thing I am?

1. *Text-contemplation*

To contemplate on the following two texts, read them attentively, much more slowly than usual. You might find that your mind gets impatient and "wants" to run forward through the words without fully digesting them. Resist this tendency. Savor each word and image, marvel at them, and notice how they give birth to a range of meanings.[6]

> *By convention sweet is sweet, bitter is bitter, hot is hot, cold is cold, color is color. But in reality, there are only atoms and the void.*

The following is from Aristotle (who lived about three generations after Democritus), from his book *De Anima* (*On the Soul*). Here he explains that Democritus believed that souls are composed of small spherical atoms, and their size and shape explain why, like atoms of fire, they are in constant movement:[7]

> *Some say that what originates movement is both predominantly and primarily soul... This is what led Democritus to say that soul is a sort of fire or hot substance. His "forms" or atoms are infinite in number. Those which are spherical he calls fire and soul, and compares them to the particles in the air which we see in shafts of light coming through windows. The mixture of seeds of all sorts he calls the elements of the whole of Nature (Leucippus gives a similar account).*
>
> *The spherical atoms he identifies with soul, because atoms of that shape are most adapted to permeate everywhere, and to set all the other atoms moving by being themselves in movement.*

2. *Visual contemplation*

After having digested Democritus' basic idea, let us now turn to the drawing which you will find in this chapter. Let your eyes float slowly over the drawing and stop gently on any detail that attracts your attention. Listen inwardly to what it might suggest to you.

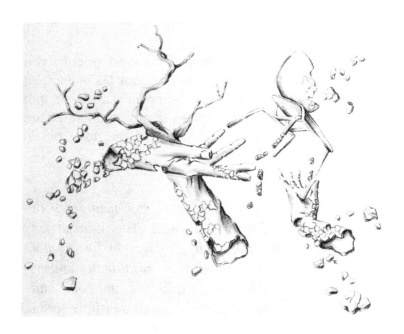

3. *Issue contemplation*

Whether or not the theory of atomism is correct, it clearly clashes with the way we experience ourselves as a single unified self. What does the fact that I experience myself as a unity tell me about myself?

Seeds of contemplation

The following "seeds of contemplation" could serve as starting points for your contemplation. Choose one of them (or compose your own) and let it grow and unfold itself in your mind.

a) The image of the **meaning-seeker**: My mind strives to make sense of itself, and it therefore tries to find – or invent – ways to connect the elements of my life into a meaningful story. My mind is a meaning-seeker. This is why I experience my life not as a collection of separate events and elements, but as one unified life-story that happens to one single person. In other words, my mind portrays my thoughts, my pains, my actions and conversations as aspects of a single unifying self.

b) The image of the **company manager**: I am made of a large number of particles, but it would be impractical, indeed impossible, to be aware of all of them. For the purpose of controlling my behavior, I only need to be aware of the main outlines of my body, of my mind and of my environment, while ignoring their many details. As a result, I am not aware of the tiny particles that compose me and my world, only of their overall configuration. I am like a company manager who is aware of the large-scale activity in the company, but not of every single worker.

c) The concept of the **spiritual seeker**: My sense of myself as a unity is a product of my spiritual yearning to find harmony and wholeness in life – in myself as well as in the world around me. Like a spiritual seeker, I seek wholeness, the All. That is why when I am in nature, I often experience harmony and beauty. And that is why I experience myself as one whole being.

Chapter 7

THE S OPHISTS – TRUTH IS RELATIVE

Introduction

In the 5th century BC, a new kind of intellectuals appeared in ancient Greece – the Sophists. These were thinkers who hired their services as professional educators, teaching public speaking, the art of argumentation, and related topics. They were not an organized school of thought, but rather individual thinkers who responded to new social conditions that produced a growing demand for public activity and political skills. As a result, they were less concerned about the truth than about the art of convincing, and less interested in developing theories than in the ability to reason in support of any given opinion, as absurd as it might seem.

The word "Sophist" came from the Greek word "Sophia" – wisdom, but as a result of their reputation it acquired negative connotations, implying somebody who twists ideas for the sake of winning an argument.

The Sophists did not have one unified philosophical theory, but it is not surprising that many of them believed that truth is relative.

One of the most prominent Sophists was Protagoras (about 490-420 BC), whose views we will examine in this chapter. Diogenes Laertius, who lived about six centuries after him, wrote: "Protagoras was the first person who demanded payment of his pupil, fixing his charge at a hundred *mine*. ... He based his arguments on words, and was the parent of the present superficial and futile kinds of discussion."[8]

Reflecting: Is truth objective?

In everyday life, we often find ourselves in disagreement about various issues: Which candidate would be best as president? Should murderers get the death penalty? How common is racism in our society? Does the business world discriminate against women? In some such cases, there is a way to determine who is right and who is wrong – for example, by carefully examining the facts, or by consulting a reliable source. But in many other cases there seems to be no conclusive evidence one way or another.

It is especially difficult to settle differences of opinion on issues of ethics, aesthetics, religion, and similar matters involving values. On such matters there is usually no neutral procedure, accepted by all sides in the debate, to determine who is right. An argument might seem convincing to one side while unconvincing to another, and as long as the two sides do not agree on how to evaluate arguments, the disagreement cannot be resolved.

All of us have probably found ourselves in such debates that seem irresolvable. But what does this show? Does it simply mean that one side in the debate is too stubborn to admit that it is mistaken? Or that in issues of values there is no right or wrong? Do we have to give up the idea of objective truth and accept that what is true for me may not be true for you?

Protagoras' response: Truth is a matter of opinion

Protagoras' writings have been lost, but on the basis of the few comments and quotations by later thinkers that survive today, it appears that he did indeed claim that in matters of values, especially in ethics and politics, there is no objective truth or falsity. The arguments that support any given belief, Protagoras declared, are equally good as the opposite arguments. It seems to follow that truth cannot be determined by any acceptable method, and it is therefore a matter of opinion, in other words relative to the individual.

This, however, does not mean that all beliefs are equally valuable. Although we have to give up the attempt to discover which of them is objectively true, we can still seek to determine which of them is more useful. For example, although it is impossible to determine whether or not generosity is a virtue in some absolute sense, we can still inquire whether generosity is a useful means for creating happiness and prosperity.

Some *key concepts* to reflect upon:

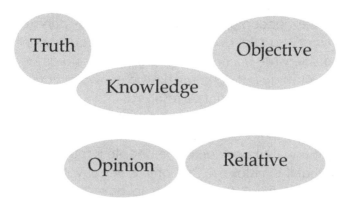

Contemplating

In today's world, Protagoras' position might not seem surprising. Like him, many people nowadays claim that in matters of values, no rational argument can determine conclusively who is right and who is wrong. Interestingly, however, this does not stop most of us from arguing over values, and from doing so quite passionately or even bitterly. We often feel virtually compelled to defend our beliefs when they are being criticized, we feel irritated when our values are being mocked, we feel the urge to show our opponents their mistakes, and we get impatient and passionate in the debate.

It may seem strange to find ourselves being so argumentative if we do not believe in an objective, universal truth. It appears that something within us rebels against our relativistic declarations and rejects the idea that truth is relative. Our values seem to be not just idle ideas that lie passively in our mind, but something more similar to a force that animates us to act with commitment and passion. And this raises the question: How should we understand this curious fact? Or more generally, what does it mean to believe in a value?

To contemplate on this issue, you may consider a personal example of a value which you feel strongly about, and which recently made you defensive or argumentative.

1. Text-contemplation

In contemplation, our mind must be fresh and attentive, and therefore as free as possible from automatic thoughts and prior opinions. If we find ourselves repeating our familiar opinions, then we are probably not fully in a contemplative state of mind.

One way to help the mind retain its openness is to slow down its normal pace in order to pull it out of its familiar thinking patterns. Thus, to contemplate on the following brief text you may copy it to your notebook attentively and carefully, writing each word very slowly and as beautifully as you can. The slow and careful writing has the power of taking the mind out of its automaticity and opening it for unexpected insights. You may also try writing the same sentence several times again and again.

As our text for contemplation, we will use Diogenes Laertius, a biographer of the Greek philosophers who lived some six centuries after Protagoras, and probably had access to some of his writings and recorded sayings. He quotes Protagoras as writing:[9]

In every question there are two arguments exactly opposite to one another.

Man is the measure of all things: of those things which exist – that they are; and of those things which do not exist – that they are not.

Concerning the gods, I am not able to know with certainty whether they exist or whether they do not. For there are many things which prevent one from knowing, especially the obscurity of the subject, and the shortness of the life of man.

2. *Visual contemplation*

Sit quietly and observe the drawing found in this chapter, letting your eyes glide slowly and gently over its different elements. If a certain aspect of the drawing intrigues you, ask yourself what it might be saying to you about the topic of truth and relativity.

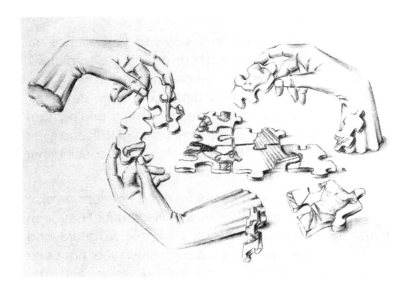

3. *Issue-contemplation*

Declarations such as "Everything is relative!" are common nowadays, yet as we have already noted, it is not easy to dismiss objective truth, because most of us care a lot about it. We usually invest effort and time and money for the sake of our convictions, and we sometimes even risk our lives for them. Evidently, we do not perceive our truths as just a matter of arbitrary personal taste. How, then, do we perceive them? How do I experience "my truth" and what does it mean to me?

Seeds of contemplation

To contemplate on this issue, we may use one of the following "seeds of contemplation" as a starting point for contemplation.

a) The metaphor of an ***inner demand***: I experience my truth not as an inert idea which I can adopt or discard at will, but as an active demand directed at me. When I truly believe in a moral value, I feel that it calls me to be faithful to it, it urges me to defend it, to keep it in mind, and perhaps display it to others. I cannot remain indifferent to it, and even when I decide to shun it, this requires from me a special inner effort, hesitation, or guilt feelings.

b) The metaphor of ***a guardian***: When I accept a value as my truth, I accept it as something precious that has been entrusted to me. By accepting it I agree to guard and nurture it, just like a precious animal or flower that has been entrusted to me. From now on I am its guardian, and I am personally responsible to protect it.

c) The concept of ***faithfulness***: My personal value is not merely an opinion, but an ideal to which I am faithful. If I believe in some value only abstractly, without any commitment or passion, then this belief is not yet a personal truth. A personal truth is a vision which animates and inspires me, and thus something that motivates me to be faithful to it.

PART B

THE ATHENIAN PHILOSOPHERS

Ancient Greece was not a single country, but divided into a number of city-states, each with its own ruler. In the fifth century BC, the city-state of Athens rose to dominance in the Greek world, in terms of wealth, power and culture. Three major philosophers appeared in the fifth and fourth centuries in ancient Athens: Socrates, his pupil Plato, and Plato's pupil Aristotle (born in Macedonia, in northern Greece, but came to Athens to study with Plato). Their philosophies, though quite different from each other, exerted a profound influence on Western thought for many centuries, especially in the Medieval and Renaissance periods. It is difficult to imagine the history of Western philosophy without them.

Chapter 8

SOCRATES – CARING FOR YOUR SOUL

Introduction

Socrates (470-399 BC) was a major philosopher of ancient Greece whose influence on the history of Western philosophy has been profound. He is known to us primarily through the writings of his students Plato and Xenophon, as well as the theater plays of Aristophanes. He lived in Athens, and was in the habit of dragging the people he encountered into philosophical discussions. He would question their beliefs about some concept – about courage, or virtue, etc., asking them for a definition of that concept. Through a dialogue made of questions and answers, he would show them that they did not know what they thought they knew.

Eventually Socrates was accused by the Athenian authorities of corrupting the youth and of impiety, and after a brief trial was found guilty, sentenced to death and taken to prison. He rejected his friends' proposals to escape, and was executed by drinking poison. His faithful disciples, among them the young man who would later become the great philosopher Plato, continued to cherish his wisdom and integrity.

Since Socrates did not write anything, we will focus in this chapter on what his student Plato wrote in his text *Apology*, which records his teacher's trial and execution. Here Plato quotes Socrates' self-defense speech in front of the Athenian court that sentenced him to death.

Reflecting: How should I care for my soul?

Unlike most people, Socrates did not bother to attain wealth, fame, political power, or even comfort and security. As he explained in his defense speech reported in Plato's *Apology*, it is more important to care for your soul than anything else. Curiously, he notes, most people care for their money or body or reputation, while neglecting their soul.

What, then, does it mean to care for your soul? And why is it so important?

Socrates' response: Knowing yourself

For Socrates, you care for your soul when you make sure that you are living a life worth living. This is an ethical life, a life of virtue, justice, and reason.

However, in order to achieve this, you must examine yourself and come to know yourself. That's because living correctly does not happen by itself. On the contrary, our automatic tendency is to seek superficial pleasures, to blindly follow the crowd, to act unthinkingly according to social norms. Living a life worth living requires knowledge and self-knowledge.

Thus, in order to care for your soul you must examine yourself, especially your beliefs and the assumptions on which they rest. You cannot take it for granted that the ideas and values which you have internalized are correct. You cannot simply assume that your automatic tendencies, your intuitions, or your common sense are dependable. You cannot be sure that what seems to you right is indeed right. You must use reason to question your ideas about life and examine them critically: What is virtue? What does it mean to be honest or courageous? What is justice? And so on.

Caring for your soul requires self-examination, and that is why Socrates says in the *Apology*: "The unexamined life is not worth living." Such self-examination is what philosophy is all about. To examine yourself is to philosophize.

*Some **key concepts** to reflect upon:*

Virtue

Care of the soul

Self-knowledge

Self-examination

Contemplating

Since for Socrates caring for your soul requires self-examination, we might wonder what exactly is meant by self-examination. There are different kinds of self-examination: examining your emotional life, examining your opinions and how reasonable they are, examining the childhood roots of your behavior, etc. What kind of self-examination is best for promoting a life worth living? Or, if they are all important, are they equally important, or are some more important than others?

Socrates favors a rational examination of one's beliefs. In his conversations he typically challenges his interlocutor to define some concept, and then subjects the proposed definition to rational scrutiny. But here we may wonder: Is a rational examination of abstract ideas an effective way to know yourself and care for your soul? Wouldn't a more personal kind of self-examination be preferrable?

To contemplate on this issue, we may consult our own life-experiences. We may thank Socrates for presenting the issue so powerfully, but it is now our turn to formulate our own understanding of what it means to examine ourselves in an effective way.

1. *Text-Contemplation*

Read Socrates' words slowly and gently, savoring them carefully. Try to discern Socrates' vision of caring for the soul and of self-examination, and reflect on how effective this vision might be.

The following is from Plato's *Apology*, which records Socrates' speech in his trial:[10]

> As long as I have life and strength I will never stop practicing and teaching philosophy, and I will exhort anyone I meet in my usual way, and explain to him, saying:

"O my friend, why do you, who are a citizen of the great and mighty and wise city of Athens, care so much about accumulating the greatest amount of money and honor and reputation, and so little about wisdom and truth and the greatest improvement of the soul, which you never consider at all? Are you not ashamed of this?"

And if the person with whom I am arguing responds: "Yes, but I do care," then I do not leave him or let him go at once. I interrogate and examine and cross-examine him, and if I think that he has no virtue, but only says that he has, I reproach him for under-valuing what is more important, and over-valuing what is less so. And this I will say to everyone I meet, young and old, citizen and alien, but especially to the citizens, since they are my brothers.

...

If I say that the greatest good of man is to converse daily about virtue, and about everything about which you hear me examining myself and others, and that the unexamined life is not worth living – you are less likely to believe me. And yet, what I say is true, although it is hard for me to persuade you.

2. Visual contemplation

Bring into your mind Socrates' idea of caring for one's soul, and then examine carefully the drawing you will find in this chapter. Get a sense of its general layout and meaning, and notice if any particular detail strikes you as intriguing or meaningful.

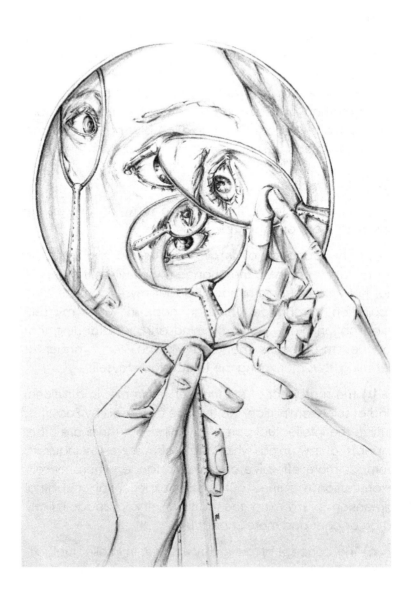

3. *Issue-Contemplation*

As already noted, Socrates' approach to self-examination employs abstract reasoning, and one might wonder whether it is the best way for self-improvement. Analyzing the universal definition of virtue, for example, might not seem to tell me much about my own personal path to virtue.

More generally, if our aim is to elevate our lives, then not every method of examining ourselves is equally valuable. Thus, our question for contemplation is: What kind of self-examination can best help us transform our way of living?

Seed of contemplation

To contemplate on this issue, we may use one of the following seeds of contemplation:

a) The concept of *inspiration for self-change*: Self-examination can help me change myself when it gives me not just impersonal information about myself, but also the inspiration to change. This can happen when my self-examination produces in my mind an understanding that touches me, shakes me, and fills me with wonder or yearning, thus motivating me to transform myself.

b) The metaphor of *the inquirer within me*: In a rational kind of self-examination, like the one proposed by Socrates, I utilize the intellectual part of my mind. But there are other aspects of my mind which can also serve as inquirers, perhaps more effective ones. For instance, when my self-examination is carried out by the experiential or spiritual dimensions of my mind, the resulting self-knowledge is likely to be deeper and more impactful.

c) The concept of *loving knowledge*: In intellectual self-examination I examine myself through thoughts and ideas. But alternatively, I can also examine myself through love. Love, too, has a sensitivity that can serve as a way of knowing. When I relate to life lovingly, I learn about myself through the experience of love, just as my fingers learn the shape of an object through the experience of touch.

Chapter 9

P LATO – THE LADDER OF LOVE

Introduction

Plato (about 428-347 BC) is undoubtedly one of the greatest philosopher in the history of Western thought. He grew up in ancient Athens, and as a young man became a student of Socrates. After Socrates' death he founded a school which became known as "The Academy," and which continued operating for hundreds of years. Among Plato's students was the great philosopher Aristotle. Many of Plato's books survived to this day, unlike the writings of other ancient philosophers which have been lost. He often wrote them in the form of a dialogue, putting his ideas in Socrates' mouth. Plato's writings greatly influenced later thinkers, especially in the Middle Ages and Renaissance.

At the heart of Plato's philosophy is the view that the material world which we perceive through our senses is only a shadow of a higher reality. It can only be grasped through a higher form of intuitive understanding.

Our soul yearns to transcend the material world and reach this higher reality. Material things – trees, animals, stones, houses, bodies, etc. – have a low level of reality because they are imperfect copies of ideal forms, or "ideas."

For example, the triangular shape of a roof is far from perfect – its sides are crooked and also thicker than precise lines. It is a triangle only because it resembles the ideal form of a triangle. The conclusion is that material things are less real than ideal forms, or ideas. Our material world as a whole is only an imperfect copy of the perfect world of ideas.

There are many perfect ideas – the idea of a triangle, the idea of a horse, and so on, but the highest of all is perfection itself. This is the idea of goodness, truth, beauty, or what Plato calls The One. Our yearning for this perfection is the Platonic "Eros" which motivates us to reach high. It also motivates us to philosophize, since philosophy is designed to lead us to higher levels of understanding, towards the One which we love. In this sense, philosophy is the art of loving.

Reflecting: What is love?

Plato's view of love can best be seen in his text *The Symposium* that describes a drinking party in which each participant has to give a speech in praise of Eros (love). Socrates is one of them, and he too gives a speech. The ideas he expresses are apparently Plato's, and Socrates' character is used only as a literary device.

In his speech, "Socrates" explains that the essence of love is the yearning for perfect and eternal beauty. In contrast, love for specific objects – for men or women, for gold, for wine, etc. – is a lower level of love, directed at lower, imperfect forms of beauty. These lower kinds of love fail to fully satisfy our soul's yearning for perfection.

But here one might wonder: If Plato is right and we yearn for absolute perfection, then how are ordinary forms of love possible at all? In everyday life we love ordinary people, pets, flowers, foods which, as material objects, have faults and limitations. The things we normally love are not perfect, certainly not absolutely and eternally. How can we possibly love them?

More generally, what is the relationship between our ordinary love of ordinary objects and our love of perfect beauty?

Plato's response: reflections of perfection

For Plato, perfect beauty is the source of the material beauty which we perceive in the material world. Therefore, although material objects do not have perfect beauty, we can vaguely sense perfect beauty through them. An object's partial beauty reflects perfect beauty somewhat like dirty blue jeans reflecting pure blueness, or a drawing of a triangle in the sand reflecting – despite its inaccuracy – the idea of a perfect geometric triangle. Likewise, the beauty of a face or a flower resembles beauty itself.

This means that there are different levels of reality: There is triangularity of a lower or imperfect level and triangularity of a higher or perfect level, and likewise low imperfect squareness and high perfect squareness, low horse-ness and high horse-ness; and similarly, lower beauty and higher beauty.

Thus, reality is organized on different levels of perfection or realness. The material objects we perceive around us have a low level of reality, but they reflect (or resemble) a higher, non-material reality. Furthermore, when we love a "low" object – a specific face or shirt or painting, what attracts us is the perfect beauty that is reflected in it. When you think you love a pair of shoes in the store-window, your soul in fact loves perfection itself; it is longing for the highest level of beauty and reality, which Plato calls "The One."

If this is so, then we are no longer discussing love as a specific emotion, but the nature of reality itself. We are not doing merely human psychology but metaphysics!

Some *key concepts* to reflect upon:

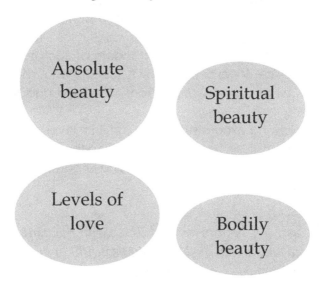

Contemplating

How is Plato's grand metaphysical vision relevant to our daily lives? Does it mean that some things in our lives are higher and worth loving, while others are lower so that our love for them is lower and less valuable? And if so, then does this mean that we should try to abandon our love for "low" things such as food and bodily pleasures, and instead try to develop higher forms of love?

To search for answers to these issues, let us contemplate on Plato's idea. The result would not necessarily be faithful to his original intentions, but historical precision is not our goal in this book. We are seeking to dialogue with great thinkers and use their vision as a starting point for our own insights.

1. *Text-contemplation*

In his *The Symposium*, Plato describes the path of love from the lowest level of love – love for a particular physical body – to the highest level of love, which is love for Beauty itself. Plato puts the words in the mouth of Socrates (as a literary device to express his own ideas), who allegedly recounts what a wise woman from Mantineia had taught him.

The following excerpts describe the final level of love for eternal Beauty itself. To contemplate, read them quietly and attentively while savoring the words and images and letting them speak within you.[11]

He who has been instructed thus far in the matters of love, and who has learned to see the beautiful in the proper order and stages, now approaches the end. He will suddenly perceive a wondrous beauty – and this, Socrates, is the final end of all his previous efforts. This beauty is, first, everlasting – not coming and going or growing and fading. And second, it is not beautiful from one point of view and ugly from another ... but is beauty only, absolute, separate, simple, and everlasting, without decrease or increase or any change. It is the beauty that is reflected in all the beautiful things.

... And the true order of progressing in the things of love is to use the beauties of material objects as steps on which to climb upwards towards that other beauty, going from one object to two objects, and from two to all beautiful forms, and from beautiful forms to beautiful actions, and from beautiful actions to beautiful ideas, until from beautiful ideas one arrives at the absolute beauty, and at last knows what the essence of beauty is.

"This, my dear Socrates," said the stranger of Mantineia, "is the life which is above all others which a person should live, in the contemplation of absolute beauty. It is a beauty which if you perceive once, you would no longer be after the allure of gold, and clothing, and pretty boys and youths which now astonish you when you look at them..."

2. Visual contemplation

Quietly scan the drawing in this chapter and note how each of the different elements in it contributes to the whole. Pay attention to the drawing's upward orientation, and reflect on what it says to you.

3. Issue-Contemplation

According to Plato, as you advance on the path to perfect beauty you acquire wisdom. Every step in the ladder of love inspires in you a higher understanding of beauty. As he says in the above quotation: "and at last he knows what the essence of beauty is."

What kind of knowledge or wisdom is this? How would it be expressed in your behavior, your state of mind, your attitude to life?

Seeds of contemplation

You are invited to use one of the following ideas as a starting point for your contemplation.

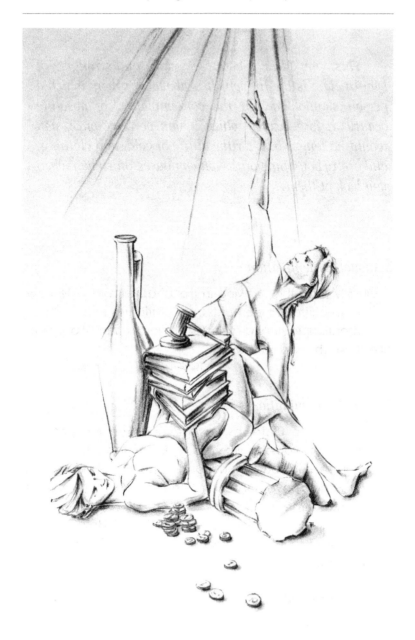

a) The metaphor of *greater horizons*: When you understand the universality of beauty and how the same beauty is reflected in all beautiful things, your mind is no longer preoccupied with this or that specific object. You no longer see the world in terms of your fragmentary experiences. Your mind now expands so that you live in constant awareness of the greater horizons of reality.

b) The metaphor of *a higher self*: After experiencing a higher beauty, you are no longer motivated by petty concerns and trivial interests. Your familiar small self is transcended, and you start living from a higher self. Your thoughts, feelings and desires come to you from a higher source – from a higher awareness that appreciates greater matters.

c) The metaphor of *a traveler returning home*: After you have experienced absolute beauty, you return to your small self and your particular concerns. But you are not the same. Like a villager who returns home after a long journey around the world, you are different from those who have never left their small village. Now you know. You may seem an ordinary villager, but inwardly you are wiser, and you often sense longing and incompleteness, as well as greater emotions which your fellow villagers cannot even imagine.

Chapter 10

ARISTOTLE – FLOURISHING

Introduction

Aristotle (384–322 BC) was one of the most prominent philosophers in the history of Western philosophy. He was born in Macedonia, as a young man went to Athens to study with Plato, and later became tutor of Alexander the Great. His writings are systematic, written mostly in the form of lecture notes, and covering virtually all the fields of knowledge that existed at the time. He wrote about metaphysics, cosmology, physics, mathematics, biology, psychology, ethics, politics and economics, aesthetics, music, poetry and theater, and these writings became basic for many centuries after him. Among other things, he developed the first systematic theory of ethics, and he invented a system of formal logic which dominated philosophy until modern times.

In sharp contrast with his teacher Plato, Aristotle did not believe in higher levels of reality (like Plato's "ideas"). His philosophy tends to be this-worldly, focused on specific aspects of life or reality, and it explores their structure systematically, sometimes on the basis of empirical observations.

The following discussion focuses on the beginning of Aristotle's *Nicomachean Ethics*, a major treatise on the principles of ethics. Here Aristotle discusses "eudaimonia," which can be translated from Greek as happiness or flourishing.

Reflecting: What is the goal of life?

Aristotle's treatise *Nicomachean Ethics* starts with the question: What is the goal of our actions in life?

Everything we do is aimed at some goal – at a "good" which we want to obtain. But some of our goals are not important in themselves; they are only means for other goals. For example, you buy a car not for the sake of owning a car, but for the sake of transportation, or perhaps in order to impress your friends – which in itself is in order to feel important. But this chain of "in order to" cannot go forever. There must be a final end that is not just a means for something else, but rather is good in itself. That is the goal of all our activities in life.

What is this final end – the highest good that we can hope to attain through our actions?

Aristotle's response: Happiness (Eudaimonia)

Aristotle responds that eudaimonia, or happiness, is the final good which is the goal of all our actions (if they are rational). Indeed, happiness is good for its own sake – it makes no sense to ask: "Why do you want to be happy?" Well, I want to be happy because I want to be happy!

But here we must be precise. Several points should be noted here:

First, eudaimonia is not exactly happiness, if by "happiness" we mean a pleasurable subjective feeling. It means, more precisely, flourishing. What we seek in life is not just to feel good at all costs – would you want to be a happy murderer, or a happy idiot? – but rather to flourish just as a tree flourishes. Good feelings are part of eudaimonia, but not all of it.

This leads to a second point: eudaimonia or happiness is not a momentary state. It is not enough to feel good for two minutes in order to count as a happy person. Happiness is a state that stretches over a long period of time, or even a whole lifetime.

Third, in order to be happy, it is not enough to think that you are happy. For example, a person who gets "high" on drugs all the time is not a happy person even if he imagines himself to be so. There are also objective criteria that determine whether or not you are in a state of happiness: the pursuit of happiness must be rational. Because, says Aristotle, rationality, or reason, is an essential part of our human nature. Flourishing as a human being does not mean flourishing as a zombie, or as a dog, but as a rational human being.

Aristotle mentions several additional elements of eudaimonia, such as having friends, a good family, luck – without them it is difficult to flourish. But perhaps the most interesting element is that eudaimonia goes together with ethics. In order to flourish in the sense of eudaimonia, you must be a virtuous person. You must be courageous, generous, honest, etc.

At this point, Aristotle starts his famous discussion on the nature of virtues. He concludes that virtue is a behavioral tendency that can be developed like a second nature that you attain through practice. Furthermore, virtue is usually the midway between extremes: courage is between cowardice and rashness, generosity is between wastefulness and stinginess, etc.

To sum up, then, happiness for Aristotle consists of rational activity in accordance with virtue throughout one's life.

Some **key concepts** to reflect upon:

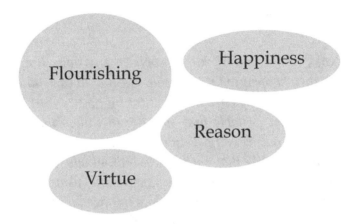

Contemplating

Aristotle's view of virtues and eudaimonia is complex, but for our purpose of personal contemplation, the above points are sufficient. Let us focus on the main concepts we have encountered – flourishing, virtue, and reason – and contemplate on how they are connected to each other.

1. *Text-contemplation*

Reflect on your own life-experience and consider how your eudaimonia or happiness connects to your ethical virtues. From your own experience, is it possible to be unethical and happy at the same time, or conversely, ethical and unhappy? Keep this issue in mind while reading quietly and slowly the following fragments from Aristotle's *Nicomachean Ethics*, letting the words speak within you:[12]

> *Happiness is something final and self-sufficient and is the goal of all actions.*
>
> *...*
>
> *Now, in the case of most people, the various things which they happen to find pleasant clash with each other, because these things are not pleasant by nature. But the lovers of what is noble find pleasure in things that are pleasant by nature. And actions that are in accordance with virtue are like that. So for these individuals, virtuous actions are both pleasant to them and pleasant in themselves. Therefore, their life does not need pleasure as an additional attraction towards virtue, because virtue already has pleasure in itself. ...*
>
> *If this is so, then virtuous actions must be in themselves pleasant. And they are certainly good and noble, and they are good and noble in the highest degree, since the good person makes good judgements in those matters. Thus, happiness is the most excellent, most noble, and most pleasant thing in life.*

2. Visual contemplation

Recalling Aristotle's notions of eudaimonia and of virtue, look at the drawing in this chapter, absorb it, and let it "speak" to you. What does the drawing suggest to you about these two concepts?

3. *Issue-Contemplation*

Aristotle's notion of "eudaimonia" combines several different elements: a subjective sense of well-being,

continuity over a period of time, flourishing, rationality, moral virtue. One might wonder: How are these elements connected to each other within the notion of eudaimonia, and what is the "glue" that binds them together? How should we envision the common essence of eudaimonia?

Seeds of contemplation

To contemplate on this question, the following ideas can serve as starting points:

a) The image of a ***flourishing tree***: I am a tree, working to develop my roots, my branches, my leaves, my fruits. Growing does not happen by itself – I must nurture myself with care and patience in order to realize my full nature as a tree. The cultivation of my natural capacities as a tree, like the cultivation of our human rationality and virtue, gives me a sense of happiness and well-being.

b) The image of ***the dancer***: Virtue, for Aristotle, is an excellence of your character, and as such it is not just a matter of how you feel or think, but mainly how you act in the world. This can be compared to dancing: You are an excellent dancer once you can express your excellence on the stage. You must know how to move with grace, to attain focus and balance, to act with precision. And when you have mastered the dance of life, you do so with joy. This is the happiness of dancing.

c) The concept of ***celebrating my humanity***: I flourish with eudaimonia when I fulfill my highest human potentials. These are not the low pleasures of drinking or the excitement of a wild party, but the sublime joy of celebrating the highest dimensions of my humanity – my excellence, my rationality, my virtues.

PART C

THE HELLENISTIC PHILOSOPHERS

After the deaths of Aristotle and of Alexander the Great, in the 4th century BC, Greece became part of larger empires, and eventually, in the first century AD, part of Rome. Ordinary people no longer lived in their own city-state and had little political influence on their society and city. Indeed, the philosophies after Aristotle often regarded the world as alien, and they recommended withdrawing into one's own inner world or minimizing involvement in society. Together these approaches are called Hellenistic philosophy, and they lasted until the rise of Christianity to dominance and the fall of Rome at the end of 4th century AD.

Although Greece lost its independence and was now absorbed into larger empires, Greek culture exerted a considerable influence on many societies around the Mediterranean and all the way to central Asia. Several important schools of philosophy flourished at that time, each one lasting for generations or centuries, notably Epicureanism, Stoicism, Neo-Platonism, Skepticism, the Peripatetic school, Cyrenaicism and Cynicism. In the following chapters we will focus on the first four.

Chapter 11

Epicurus – TRUE AND FALSE NEEDS

Introduction

Epicurus (341–270 BC) was a Greek philosopher who founded so-called Epicureanism, an important school of thought in the Hellenistic period. When he was in his thirties he bought a house with a garden outside Athens, where he and his followers spent peaceful time together and conversed. This was the legendary "Garden of Epicurus."

Epicurus envisioned the world as composed of material facts, somewhat similar to modern science. He believed that nature is made of atoms, that there is no soul, and that death is the end of our existence. He is famous for his teaching that the goal of life is what he called "pleasure," by which he meant a quiet state of mind that is free of any kind of suffering, including anxiety, agitation and frustration. In this kind of life we avoid excessive desires and satisfy our basic needs, such as basic foods and clothing, friendship, and conversing and philosophizing together. Epicurus' philosophy influenced many thinkers throughout the ages.

Reflecting: What is a true need?

"I need a new car!" says a husband to his wife.

"You mean you *desire* a new car – you don't really need it. Our old car is perfectly fine."

"But can you imagine the neighbors' admiration when they see us in a new red sports car?"

"That's not a need, that's a fantasy!"

This little dialogue demonstrates that what you *think* you need is not necessarily what you truly need. Consider the many things you pursue or covet in everyday life – new fancy clothes and jewelry, restaurants and parties, travels, money and power. Do you really "need" all of these things?

More generally, what counts as a true need, as opposed to an imaginary or false need? This is the issue which Epicurus raised, and which he regarded as crucial for a happy life. The problem in answering this question, Epicurus believed, is that most people do not understand what they really need. The role of philosophy is to help them find the answer.

Epicurus' answer: True needs promote "pleasure"

Epicurus' answer is: A desire expresses a true need if it can help you attain what is valuable in life. False needs are desires that do not help you attain it, and may even interfere with it.

So what is valuable in life?

According to Epicurus, the most valuable quality in life is pleasure. A good life is a life of pleasure. However, by "pleasure" he does not mean wild parties of wine and passion (as his opponents accused him), because he defines pleasure as the absence of pain. Thus, a good life is a quiet life that is free from distress, pain, and excessive excitement. It is guided by reason and moderation and avoids anything which might cause agitation and distress, such as the race for success and money, craving fancy clothes and food, lust and debauchery.

What are the needs that promote such a life? The minimum to keep you comfortable and safe. Anything beyond minimal comfort and security is excessive. You truly need a place to live, some clothes to wear, enough food to avoid hunger, but not much more. Simple food, clothes and lodgings are enough – any extravagance would be superfluous, and thus destructive to your well-being. In addition, you need to maintain pleasurable activity throughout the day, which for Epicurus means primarily friends to keep you company and philosophical conversations.

Most people, however, want more. They want to be rich or successful, to wear expensive clothes, to own many things, to have fun and excitement. They are driven by false needs which do not contribute to the quiet pleasurable life that is so valuable. Philosophy can show them their mistake.

Some *key concepts* to reflect upon:

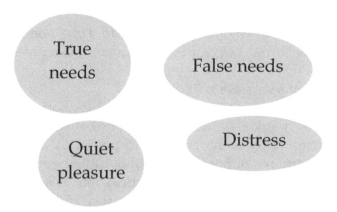

Contemplating

Epicurus' ideas challenge the culture of consumerism and of the race for success which are promoted by contemporary society, and which most of us share to one extent or another. Let us reflect on the alternative which he suggests: Imagine that you were given the opportunity to live with your friends in a quiet retreat house, like Epicurus' Garden, without the need to work for a living, provided you lead a simple and quiet Epicurean life. What would it be like for you to live so simply and pleasantly for a period of time? And which capacities or sensitivities would you have to cultivate in yourself in order to flourish in this kind of lifestyle?

1. *Text-contemplation*

Read slowly and carefully the following text, which describes the Epicurean way of life. Try placing yourself in this kind of life and sensing the inner attitude that it requires. The text is taken from Epicurus' "Letter to Menoeceus":[13]

The goal of all our actions is to be free from pain and fear, and once we have attained all this, the storm of the soul quiets down, since the living creature has no need to go in search of something that is lacking, nor to look for anything else to fulfill the good of the soul and of the body. That is why we call pleasure the beginning and end of the good life.

...

> *Whatever is natural is easily provided, while vain and worthless pleasures are hard to obtain. Simple food gives as much pleasure as a luxurious diet, once the pain of need has been removed, while bread and water give the highest pleasure when they are brought to hungry lips. Therefore, getting used to simple and inexpensive diet is all that is needed for health, and it enables a person to meet the necessary requirements of life.*

2. *Visual contemplation*

While keeping in mind the notions of false needs, true needs, and Epicurean pleasure, slowly inspect this drawing and try to discern what it suggests to you.

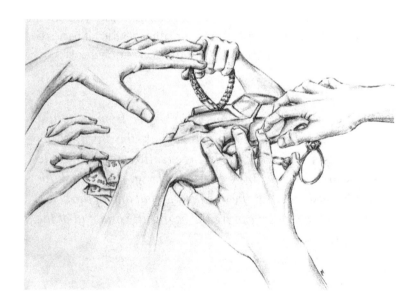

3. Issue-Contemplation

Whether or not you accept Epicurus' goal of "pleasure," you can still ask yourself whether your desires express true needs or false needs. Whether you value fun, or wisdom, or love or something else, or a combination of several things, you may wonder whether your desires help you reach these values.

Consider how much time you spend on your smartphone, or gossiping, or working overtime for extra money – are all these necessary? Think of the energy you spend on trying to make a good impression on others, or on non-essential projects. Think about the money you spend on buying unnecessary gadgets, replacing old items with new ones, or going to restaurants. You will probably find that many of these things do not lead to what you consider most valuable. Evidently, we spend much of our time and resources on false needs.

Hence our question for contemplation: What does our preoccupation with false needs – in other words, non-essential desires – tell us about our human nature? To put it concretely, imagine that a group of aliens from outer space came to earth to watch humanity, and they noticed our preoccupation with desires that seem extravagant and unnecessary. What would they conclude about human nature?

Seeds of contemplation

To contemplate on this question, the following seeds of ideas might help you develop your thoughts:

a) The metaphor of **the psychological prisoner**: We are controlled by our psychological patterns of thought and behavior, which divert our attention away from our true needs. Our psychological mechanisms make us want more and more, while distracting us from important things. Thus, we are prisoners of the automatic powers that control our mind, and we often lose touch with our true needs.

b) The metaphor of ***the agave plant***: We humans are like the agave plant that blooms every several years. We cannot produce wonderful flowers continuously, we cannot follow our true needs all the time. Life is complex and it requires many things – including relaxation, mindless errands, silly pleasures, social meetings. Yet, as long as we manage to act from our true needs every once in a while, perhaps once a day or even once a week, then our life is fulfilled, just as one rare agave flower gives fulfillment to the entire life of the plant.

c) The concept of ***the preciousness of fun and excitement***: The fact that people seek fun and excitement shows, contrary to Epicurus' views, that these are important qualities in human life. Eating exotic food, wild partying, watching funny TV shows, buying fancy clothes and expensive jewelry – these evidently add to the quality of life. And if so, then there is no need to deny myself of them and suppress my desires for them with special Epicurean exercises. My desires are healthy and valuable as they are.

Chapter 12

THE STOICS – MY TRUE SELF

Introduction

Stoicism was a major Hellenistic school of philosophy which flourished from the 3rd century BC until the rise of Christianity to power in the 4th century AD. It included several influential thinkers, among them Seneca (4 BC–65 AD), Epictetus (50-135 AD), and Marcus Aurelius (121-180 AD).

Stoic philosophy consisted of many branches of knowledge, but its greatest influence and fame came from its vision of how life should be lived. For the Stoics, everything that happens in the world is determined by the universal Logos, or reason. The only place where freedom resides is in the human soul. Usually, however, we do not exercise our freedom because we let ourselves be controlled by psychological forces such as desires, passions, and attachments. As a result, we often find ourselves frustrated, angry or agitated.

The Stoic's goal was to attain inner freedom from these psychological forces and maintain inner peace and equanimity towards whatever happens to us. To achieve this, the Stoics believed, we must cultivate our inner center, which is the rational faculty within us. When we act from this inner faculty, we are rational, free, and in harmony with the Logos that governs the cosmos.

Reflecting: What is my true self?

In everyday life we talk about "me" or "I" in several different senses. In the broadest sense, "I" include my body (for example, when I say: "I am sitting at the table" or "I am tall"), my work ("I am a teacher"), and even my possessions ("I am a landowner"). But from the Stoic perspective, this is an inaccurate way of speaking, because what characterizes me is my unique nature as a human being, which is my inner being, and not my body or bodily activity which animals also have.

In a narrower sense, I am my psychological self – my feelings and thoughts, my intentions and anxieties and hopes. But from the Stoic perspective, this sense is too broad as well, because it includes elements which are not my own doings – they come from automatic tendencies or reactions ("I was scared" or "I felt jealous"), and some of them are beyond my control ("My foot hurts").

For the Stoics, what is not in my complete control is not really mine. It does not represent me as a free and rational actor, which is my unique character as a human being. What is uncontrollable *happens* to me, but it is not truly me. The true self must be a source of free thought and action. But what is this true self?

The Stoic Response: My guiding principle

According to the Stoics, the world is a cosmos – a harmonious whole in which every detail is precisely as it should be, and everything behaves according to its nature: The tree grows according to its tree-nature, and the river flows according to the nature of water. If you, as a modern reader, don't see the harmony in the world, if you think that the world is cruel and irrational, that is because you look at it from your narrow, self-centered perspective. You are like a little ant that complains about its hard work. But from the broader perspective of a biologist, the life of an anthill, including its challenges and disasters, is a marvelous piece of natural harmony. The same applies to a human being. Your personal life may seem tainted with sickness and misfortune, but even this is part of the overall cosmic harmony.

Thus, in the Stoic cosmos everything happens precisely as it should, according to the cosmic Logos that governs it. Your environment, your body, your psychology – all of these happen by necessity, with no room for chance or freedom.

However, within this cosmic ocean of necessity, there is a tiny bubble of freedom in each human soul. Your true self is this bubble of freedom, and you are free to cultivate or abuse it. The Stoics called it the "daemon" or "guiding principle" or "commanding faculty" to indicate that it has the power of directing your actions and life.

This true self within us can make free choices, although the outcomes of these choices are not always foreseeable because of external circumstances beyond our control, such as accidents, sickness, and the behavior of others. Nevertheless, although we are not free to determine the conditions outside us, we are free to control our inner reactions to those conditions. For example, we may be unable to avoid a car accident, but we are free to decide how to react to it when it happens: with anger and frustration, or alternatively with calm and inner peace. This is, indeed, the goal of the Stoic way of life – to awaken the true self within us and thus act rationally, freely and calmly.

*Some **key concepts** to reflect upon:*

Reason

The self

Cosmos

Freedom

Tranquility

Contemplating

The Stoics understood that our true self, or guiding principle, is often overcome by psychological distortions, such as our irrational expectations and desires, misguided emotions, or attachment to security and comfort. Therefore, we must constantly exercise our self and strengthen it if we want to liberate it from these psychological distortions. The Stoics devised a variety of such exercises, including regularly reminding yourself how you should behave, envisioning your place in the vast cosmos, preparing yourself for possible disasters, and similar exercises.

Even with those exercises, however it is clear that in different moments of our life we are more or less centered, more or less free from desires and fears, more or less in possession of our inner freedom. Let us ask ourselves the following questions for contemplation: What is it like to be connected to my inner center (or guiding principle)? What exactly is this state of connectedness? And how can I cultivate it?

1. *Text-contemplation*

Read the following text gently, letting the words and images float in your mind like clouds in the sky, without trying to impose on them your opinions or analyses. This exercise is called "free floating contemplation." Try to sense in your imagination what your inner "daemon" feels like, and note if new insights appear in your mind.

We will use here several fragments from *Meditations*, an influential book by the Stoic philosopher and Roman Emperor Marcus Aurelius, in which he recorded his personal thoughts and exercises. [14]

From Book 2, Section 17:

Everything which belongs to the body is a stream, and what belongs to the soul is a dream and vapor, and life is a warfare and a stranger's sojourn, and after fame comes oblivion. What, then, is that which is able to conduct a person? One and only one thing: philosophy.

But this consists in keeping the daemon within you free from violence and unharmed, superior to pains and pleasures, doing nothing without a purpose, nor falsely and with hypocrisy ... and, finally, waiting for death with a cheerful mind, as being nothing else than a dissolution of the elements of which every living being is composed.

From Book 12, Section 3:

> *There are three things of which you are composed: a little body, a little breath [life], and intelligence. Of these, the first two are yours only in the sense that it is your duty to take care of them, but only the third is properly yours.*
>
> *Therefore, you should separate from yourself – that is, from your understanding – whatever others do or say, and whatever you yourself did or said in the past, and whatever future things trouble you because they may happen, and whatever is in the body which envelopes you or in the breath [life] associated with the body ... and whatever happens in the vortex of events around you, so that your intellectual power which is exempt from fate can live pure and free by itself, doing what is just, and accepting what happens, and saying the truth ...*
>
> *Then you will be able to pass that portion of life which remains for you until your death, free from perturbations, nobly, and obedient to your own daemon.*

2. *Visual contemplation*

Think of your own guiding principle, or daemon, within you that is free from psychological forces and can make free choices with tranquility and reason. Silently inspect the drawing in this chapter and reflect on what it tells you about you and your freedom.

3. *Issue-Contemplation*

If the Stoics were right that we have a true self that can guide us to live freely, peacefully and rationally, then how can we cultivate it?

Seeds of contemplation

To contemplate on this question, we may begin with one of the following seeds of contemplation, as a starting point for developing our own insights:

a) The concept of **weakness of the will**: The reason I often lose touch with my true self is that I am weak. I may be too tired or lazy, or I may not have sufficient determination to return to my inner self and obey it. In order to overcome this situation, I should exercise my will power daily, just as I exercise my body: I should choose challenging tasks and force myself to perform them. Little by little I will make them harder and harder so as to strengthen my will power.

b) The metaphor of **learning to listen inwardly**: My true self always tries to guide me to live appropriately, but I rarely hear it. My mind is full of distractions, and my inner cacophony drowns the voice of my true self. Therefore, I should train myself to sit peacefully every day and listen inwardly to the voice of my true self.

c) The image of **the gardener and the young tree**: My true self is fragile. Like a young tree, it is vulnerable to external forces – to the winds and the sun and the rains. Therefore, I should cultivate it like a good gardener by protecting it and nurturing it carefully. This means that I should not expose my true self to difficult conditions until it grows and matures and becomes stronger. Until then, I should let it do only simple tasks, and support and encourage it.

Chapter 13

N EOPLATONISM – THE DIVINE WITHIN

Introduction

Neoplatonism (or Neo-Platonism) was a major school of philosophy that flourished in late antiquity. Neoplatonists regarded themselves as followers of Plato (who had died centuries earlier), but in fact they went much beyond his philosophy and introduced new ideas. Their influence on later philosophy, especially in the Medieval and Renaissance periods, was profound. The most famous and influential Neoplatonist was the philosopher Plotinus (204-270 AD). Other important Neoplatonists included Plotinus' student Porphyry (224-305 AD), Porphyry's student Iamblichus (245-325 AD), and Proclus (412-485 AD).

Despite differences between different Neoplatonist thinkers, for our purpose two central ideas, common to most of them, are especially worth noting: First, the idea that reality is organized on several different levels, one below the other, from the most real and spiritual level at the top, down to the lowest, material world at the bottom.

The second idea to be noted is that our goal in life, as human beings, is to transcend the material world to higher levels of reality and unify with the highest one possible.

Different Neoplatonists envisioned differently the way to transcend the material world. Plotinus emphasized meditation, philosophical reflection, and detachment from the material world. Porphyry emphasized a life of virtue and purity, at least at the beginning of the journey. Others added prayer to the gods, which were viewed as intermediary energies between the material world and highest spiritual level. Beyond these differences, all Neoplatonic philosophies have a "vertical" orientation, in the sense that they focus on the relationship between higher and lower levels of reality.

Reflecting: What is the divine element in me?

In his essay "On the life of Plotinus," Porphyry wrote about his great teacher Plotinus: "The goal of his life was, above all, to unite with the divine. And four times during the period I was with him, he achieved this union."[15]

In the same essay, Porphyry also tells us about Plotinus' last words before his death: "I am striving to give back the Divine in myself to the Divine in the All."[16] Or, in another translation: "Strive to bring back the God in yourselves to the God in the All."

This, then, is the ultimate goal of Neoplatonist philosophy. We philosophize not out of intellectual curiosity, but out of a deep yearning to get in touch with the divine element within us and elevate it to its divine source.

But what does it mean finding "the god in me" or "the divine element in me"?

In order to sharpen the question, let us recall that for Plotinus, reality is organized in several levels, the most perfect and divine at the top, and the crudest at the bottom. At the top is "The One" – the perfect unity which is beyond all concepts and thought, and which contains no division or change. At the bottom is the material world which we perceive around us, the world of bodies, shapes and colors, movement and growth and decay. Between the highest and the lowest, there are two intermediate levels – "Nous" (or Intellect) and Soul, although later Neoplatonists added additional levels. Each level of reality emerges from, or "emanates" from the reality above it, so that the One is the source of all.

To summarize, for Plotinus the series of emanations is:

(1) The One,

(2) Nous (the Intellect at the foundation of existence, which is also the realm of intuitive understanding),

(3) Soul (the soul of the cosmos, which also contains individual human souls).

(4) The material world, which is crude and base.

Normally we live on the lowest level – the material world. We identify ourselves with our body and we immerse ourselves in our material environment. But our true goal is to connect the divine element within us with higher levels of reality, and eventually with the One.

And now we can return to our question: If I, as an embodied human being, live in the material world, then what is the divine element within me?

The Neoplatonic response: My divine source

For the Neoplatonists, the divine One is not a "thing" outside me, nor is it a religious "father in heaven." It is not somebody who loves me or protects me or listens to my prayers – it is not a "somebody" at all. It is, rather, the primordial unity which is the source of all of reality, similar to

Plato's "The Good, the True, the Beautiful". From this highest level, reality
emanates downwards to lower and lower levels through a series of emanations.

Emanation does not mean that one level of reality "creates" another level, as the Biblical God created the world. It is not an act that happens at a particular time, or that requires a special intention or effort. Emanation means, rather, that one level of reality expresses itself in a lesser reality, somewhat as an object casts a shadow that is less real than the original.

This means that the divine One is my ultimate origin. Indeed, there is something divine within me, but it is distant from its source and is imprisoned in a low, base "shadow" so to speak. Our human yearning to the divine is the yearning to find the divine element within us and return it to its source.

Some *key concepts* to reflect upon:

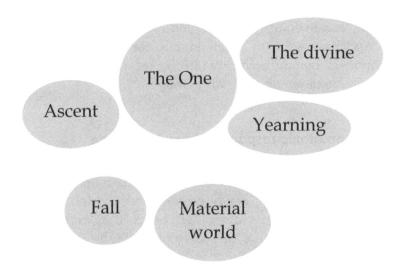

Contemplating

Let us contemplate on the Neoplatonic idea that there is a higher, divine element within me. What is it like to experience this element, and how do I find it? We may contemplate on this issue in a personal way, translating and even modifying Neoplatonic ideas to our own personal experience and self-understanding.

1. *Text-contemplation*

In the following passage by Plotinus we find him describing his own experience of rising and falling:[17]

Often I am lifted out of the body into myself, and I become external to all other things and centered in myself, and I behold a marvelous beauty. Then, more than ever, I am certain that I belong to the loftiest order. I realize the noblest life, I become one with the divine, I am stationed within it. Having reached that activity, I am placed above anything in the Intellectual realm that is less than the Supreme.

Yet, there comes the moment of descent from intuitive ("intellectual") understanding to reasoning. So after having been to the divine, I ask myself: How could it happen that I am descending now, and how did the soul ever enter into my body, the soul which, even when it is within the body is such a high thing, as it has shown itself to be?

In a later section of the same tractate, Plotinus answers his own question: My soul falls back to the material world because it is also responsible for managing my body. And when it descends from the "intellectual" realm of spiritual holistic understanding down to the material realm, it forgets its true source:

> *The individual souls have a power to administer the lower realm of their material body. They are like the sunlight that is attached above to the sun, but also takes care of what lies beneath.*
>
> *As long as the souls are with the intellectual realm, they remain whole and free from care and trouble. But there comes a stage when the souls descend from the universal to the material world, and then they become partial and self-centered. When this state continues for a while, the soul becomes a deserter from the All. It is now a partial thing, isolated, weakened, full of worries, preoccupied with the fragment, disconnected from the whole. It dwells in one body, caring only for it. ...*
>
> *Yet, even in its fallen state, the soul always has something transcendent in it. By converting itself towards the intellective act, it is freed from the chains, and it flies up, when it makes its memories the starting point of a new vision of essential being.*

2. *Visual contemplation*

Gently inspect the drawing that appears in this chapter and try to discern what it tells you about the higher element within you.

3. *Issue-Contemplation*

Even if the complex Neoplatonic worldview seems foreign to you, you may still agree that some element within you is higher, more true or divine than the rest of you. Sometimes it is easier to note the sacred element in another person, and by analogy you may conclude that you, too, have such an element.

But if so, how can I discover this divine element and connect to it?

Seeds of contemplation

To contemplate on this question, you may use one of the following seeds of contemplation as a starting point:

a) The image of **purifying my lens**: Only a pure mind can receive light from sublime sources. A dirty lens blocks the light, and my mind is too "dirty" with triviality, greed, jealousy, anger and the like. I must therefore purify my mind from every blemish and vice before trying to discern the divine and connect to it. This is a long and difficult road.

b) The concept of **philosophical remembering**: The knowledge of my divine source is inside me, but I have forgotten it. My mind is too preoccupied with practical matters, such as conversations and daily tasks, and it has forgotten where it came from. I need to stop and remind myself of the higher dimensions of life. This can be done, as Plotinus explains, by philosophizing on the big issues of existence. Philosophizing, then, is a reminder of who we are and where we belong.

c) The image of **learning the divine language**: The divine speaks in me, but my mind cannot understand it. That's because my mind does not know its language — it can understand only the language of everyday matters. In order to comprehend the divine voice, I must devote myself to listening to the voices that arise in my mind. At first I will not understand them, but little by little I will learn their language.

Chapter 14

THE SKEPTICS – CAN I EVER BE SURE?

Introduction

The Skeptic school of philosophy was founded by the Greek philosopher Pyrrho in the 4th-3rd century BC, and it flourished for several centuries alongside other schools such as Stoicism, Epicureanism, and Neoplatonism. The Skeptics' main goal was to achieve Ataraxia, which is a state of tranquility and absence of perturbation. This is not just a momentary experience but a general state of mind, which must be cultivated through repeated exercises. For the Skeptics, our beliefs or judgments are the main reason why we are anxious and perturbed, and for this reason they sought to suspend them and attain peace of mind. Hence, they practiced skepticism about all beliefs.

In this chapter we will focus on one Skeptic philosopher, Sextus Empiricus, who lived towards the end of the Hellenistic period, in the second-third centuries AD. He was also a physician who belonged to the medical school called "Empiricism," and that is why he is called "Empiricus." His writings are our main source of knowledge about the ancient school of Skepticism, but about his life almost nothing is known, not even where and when exactly he lived.

Reflecting: Can I trust what I think I know?

Consider the many things you think you know. Presumably you know your own name and the name of your city, you know which day of the week it is today, you know that the sun is now rising, you know the color of your dog, and so on. However, the Skeptic philosopher would ask you, how sure are you of those things? Isn't it possible that you are mistaken about them? It is conceivable that your memory betrays you (It's actually Tuesday today, not Wednesday), or that you are confused (You are mistaking the streetlight for the sun), that you are under an odd illusion (Your love for your dog influences your perception of it). You may even be suffering from some psychological disorder or be manipulated by a secret criminal organization (Your true name has been erased from your brain and a false name implanted instead).

You might object that this is highly unlikely. "The chances that I am mistaken are very slim."

That might be true, the Skeptic could reply (although how can you be sure that the chances are slim?), but the point is that you cannot be absolutely sure in your beliefs. It is conceivable – perhaps not very likely but still conceivable – that they are mistaken.

If you are not absolutely sure, according to the Skeptic, then you don't really know. You may know for sure what you think, but you can never know for sure whether your thoughts are true.

Now, if we agree with the Skeptic conclusion, then what follows? Practically speaking, should we stop trusting our ordinary beliefs about the world around us?

Sextus Empiricus' Response: Suspend all beliefs

Sextus Empiricus, like other Skeptics, contends that the beliefs we have about the world around us cannot count as knowledge. But this, he says, is not necessarily bad. These beliefs are the main reason why we are agitated. We are worried because we believe we are not making enough money, or because we believe that the boss dislikes us, or we are torn between two conflicting beliefs. Therefore, once we give up our beliefs and no longer worry about them, we will experience relief and peace.

More precisely, the Skeptics distinguished between two kinds of beliefs – those that come from direct experience and those that come from judgement. What we experience directly (for example, "I now feel pain") cannot be doubted, since we know for sure what we feel. But our judgements (for example, "Heat causes headache") are not evident since they are conceivably false, and they should be avoided.

Thus, through the suspension of beliefs (judgements) – an act which the Skeptics called *Epoché* – our mind attains quietude, or what they called *Ataraxia*. In this state we no longer worry about anything, because we assume nothing.

As Sextus Empiricus explains, in order to convince the mind to let go of its beliefs, the Skeptics developed a series of arguments designed to counter any statement and show that its opposite is equally convincing. For example, against the judgement "It is hot now" the Skeptics argued that it is based on human sensitivities, but for heat-loving animals it is cold now. This means that this judgement cannot be taken as objectively true.

*Some **key concepts** to reflect upon:*

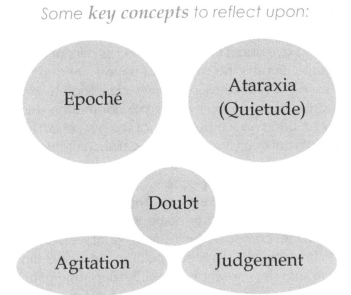

Contemplating

Are the Skeptics right that the suspension of our beliefs can lead to peace of mind?

Let us think about this issue in a less extreme manner. Let us consider not the suspension of *all* our beliefs, but *some* of our beliefs. Consider situations in which you are tense and anxious, and all kinds of worries pass through your mind and disturb your peace. Imagine that you had a technique that would make many of these beliefs disappear from your mind. Would this help to pacify you? And, more generally, what would the suspension of beliefs do to your state of mind?

1. *Text-contemplation*

Keep in mind the above questions while quietly reading the following passages, adapted from Sextus Empiricus' book *Outlines Of Pyrrhonism*.[18]

> *As soon as the Skeptic began to philosophize, he wished to discriminate between ideas and to understand which are true and which are false, in order to attain Ataraxia. He encountered, however, contradictions of equal weight, and being unable to judge, he suspended his judgement. And while his judgment was in suspension, Ataraxia followed, as if by chance, regarding matters of opinion.*
>
> *Because he who is of the opinion that anything is either good or bad by nature is always troubled. And when he does not possess those things that seem to him good, he thinks that he is tortured by the things which are by nature bad, and he pursues those that he thinks to be good. When he acquires them, however, he falls into greater perturbation, because he is excited beyond reason and without measure, fearing that his situation will change, and he does everything in his power to retain the things that seem to him good.*
>
> *In contrast, he who is undecided regarding which things are good or bad by nature, neither seeks nor avoids anything eagerly, and he is therefore in a state of Ataraxia.*

2. *Visual contemplation*

How can the Skeptic attitude be expressed in a drawing? How is it possible to illustrate the "I don't know" in shapes on paper? Lines are necessarily more definite and clear than what is unknowable. Yet, a drawing can give us the spirit of doubt, and suggest ways to understand it non-verbally.

3. *Issue-contemplation*

Consider how your mind is normally full of ideas and opinions. If you could get rid of many of them, or at least put them to sleep, would you be a better person, and would your life be a better life? To put it differently, is freedom from ideas and beliefs (or at least many of them) a good thing which we should strive to attain?

Seeds of contemplation

Here are some seeds of contemplation that might help you as starting points for your contemplation:

a) The image of a **sacred temple**: Certain kinds of beliefs are obviously necessary to survive: where to buy food, on which side of the road you should drive, where you live, etc. But beyond this minimum, cluttering the mind with many beliefs and thoughts tends to cheapen and trivialize them. Nurturing a small number of thoughts or beliefs would make us realize that they are wondrous things, precious and worth savoring. We should regard our mind not as a working machine, but as a sacred temple.

b) The concept of a **healthy mind**: Just as our body must be exercised to maintain its well-being, so must our mind. Some psychologists tell us that the mind should regularly engage in thinking activity, or else its capacities deteriorate. Whether or not this is correct is a scientific issue, but philosophically speaking, the point is that contrary to the Skeptic approach, what is most important in life is not to achieve worry-free tranquility, but rather to develop an active, inquisitive, healthy mind.

c) The concept of **the virtue of simplicity**: When you engage yourself in theorizing and analyzing, you tend to become more sophisticated. Sophistication might be a useful tool for achieving certain practical goals, but it also changes who you are. As you become more sophisticated, your attitude towards others and towards life changes too, and with it your personality. You now become calculated, manipulative, goal-oriented, and you lose your direct connection with your life and your world. Simplicity is therefore a moral virtue, and to achieve it you should free your mind from excessive thinking.

NOTES

For the sake of ease of contemplation, many quotations in this book have been slightly edited, especially to modernize old-style choice of words and sentence-structure. In addition, some fragment numbers have been changed to agree with the numbering commonly used today.

1. Adapted from Burnet, John. *Early Greek Philosophy.* 2nd ed., London, Adam and Charles Black, 1908, p. 54.

2. Adapted from Patrick, G.T.W. *The Fragments of the Work of Heraclitus of Ephesus on Nature.* Baltimore, Murray, 1889, pp. 88-101.

3. Adapted from Burnet, John. *Early Greek Philosophy.* 2nd ed., London, Adam and Charles Black, 1908, pp. 197-199.

4. Adapted from Leonard, William Ellery. *The Fragments of Empedocles.* Chicago, Open Court, 1908, pp. 21-25.

5. Adapted from Burnet, John. *Early Greek Philosophy.* 2nd ed., London, Adam and Charles Black, 1908, p. 301.

6. Adapted from Bakewell, Charles M. *Source Book in Ancient Philosophy.* 2nd ed., New York, Charles Scribner's Sons, 1909, p. 60.

7. Aristotle, *De Anima*, 1-2. Adapted from Ross, W. D. and Smith, J. A. *The Works of Aristotle*, Vol 3. Oxford, Clarendon Press, 1910.

8. Diogenes Laertius, *The Lives and Opinions of Eminent Philosophers*, Book 9, Ch. 8. Adapted from translation by C.D. Yonge, London, Bell and Sons, 1915, pp. 399.

9. *Ibid.*, pp. 397-398.

10. Plato, *Apology*, 29, 38. Adapted from Long, George. *The Apology, Phaedo and Crito of Plato.* New York, Collier, 1909, pp. 16-25.

11. Plato, *Symposium*, 211, b-c. Adapted from Jowett, Benjamin. *The Dialogues of Plato*, 2nd edition. Oxford, Clarendon Press, 1875, Vol. 2, pp. 61-62.

12. Aristotle, *Nicomachean Ethics*, Book 1, 7-8, 1097b, 1099a. Adapted from Chase, D.P. *The Nicomachean Ethics of Aristotle*. London, Dent & Sons, 1915, pp 11-15.

13. Adapted from Hicks, Robert Drew. *Stoic and Epicurean*. New York, Scribner, 1910, pp. 170-171.

14. Marcus Aurelius, Meditations, Book 2, 17 and Book 12, 3. Adapted from Long, George. *The Meditations of Marcus Aurelius*. London, Blackie & Son, 1910, Book 2, p. 20; Book 12, pp.167-168.

15. Porphyry, *Life of Plotinus*, section 2. In Mackenna, Stephen. *The Essence of Plotinus: Extracts from the Six Enneads and Porphyry's Life of Plotinus*. New York, Oxford University Press, 1934, p. 3.

16. Porphyry, *Life of Plotinus*, section 23. *Ibid.*, p. 20.

17. Plotinus, *Ennead* 4, Tractate 8, 1 and 4. Adapted from *Ibid.*, pp. 146-149.

18. Adapted from Patrick, Mary Mills. *Sextus Empiricus and Greek Scepticism*. Cambridge, Deighton Bell, 1899, p. 110.